FirstDays of the Year

E⌶

EMERGENT LITERATURES

Emergent Literatures is a series of international scope that makes available, in English, works of fiction that have been ignored or excluded because of their difference from established models of literature.

HÉLÈNE CIXOUS

FirstDays of the Year

Translated and

with a Preface by

Catherine A. F. MacGillivray

University of Minnesota Press *Minneapolis • London*

Originally published as *Jours de l'an,* copyright 1990 by Les Éditions des femmes, Paris.

Published by the University of Minnesota Press
111 Third Avenue South, Suite 290
Minneapolis, MN 55401-2520
http://www.upress.umn.edu

Cixous, Hélène, 1937–
     [Jours de l'an. English]
     Firstdays of the year / Hélène Cixous ; translated and with a preface by Catherine A. F. MacGillivray.
     p.   cm. — (Emergent literatures)
ISBN 0-8166-2116-0 (hc : alk. paper.) — ISBN 0-8166-2117-9 (pb : alk. paper)
     I. MacGillivray, Catherine A. F.   II. Title.   III. Series.
PQ2663.I9J6813   1998
843'.914—dc21   98-9302

Printed in the United States of America on acid-free paper

The University of Minnesota is an equal-opportunity educator and employer.

10 09 08 07 06 05 04 03 02 01 00 99 98   10 9 8 7 6 5 4 3 2 1

Contents

Translator's Preface

Translating Hélène Cixous's
Book of Days

Hélène Cixous's poetic fiction *Jours de l'an,* presented here in English translation, was published in France in 1990. In this essay I propose to describe for the reader, from my point of view as translator, certain characteristics of this particular example of Cixous's *écriture,* in a necessarily partial effort at illuminating what her exuberant, exasperating writing is like to work with, from where it proceeds, and what its directions tend to be.

For Cixous, as for certain other twentieth-century writers, the particularity of poetic language rests to some extent in its tendency to create, rather than to clear up, linguistic and philosophical ambiguities, and this is seen as its strength. According to Cixous, a poetic text—and we are informed early on that *FirstDays* is related to "the species of the poem," for, "poems, too, are of this astral nature, sparks as they are of a dead or distantly imminent fire"—explores a different relation to language from fiction or philosophy; in short, it thinks differently, thereby teaching us as its readers to think differently, too.

Thinking is one of the most hypnotic things we do; we think without fully understanding how it is we think. *FirstDays* limns the rhythms of a mind thinking, tentatively following, at oblique angles, each thought, each memory of the narrative voice, from its enigmatic beginnings through all its twists and turns unto the next, mysterious inception of a thought. It is a text written from the point of view of a radical subjectivity, a "subjectivity inhabited by turbulence . . . a mute struggle between the *given* subject and the subject that *surges forth,*" to quote Charles Grivel, one that dispenses with prior notions of the novel as narrative, or of poetry defined as a series of self-contained poems.[1] Furthermore, Cixous's temporality is that of the instant, of the present, not that of the sequence we associate with traditional narrative or philosophy. An economy of the instant is, it seems to me, somewhat akin to the visual, in that, as when we view a painting, we may begin reading a Cixous text on any page. As Cixous has written of the work of Clarice Lispector: "There are fifty possible ways of entering this text; it is up to the reader to find them. In terms of a quest, we can set out in many different directions. What counts is finding ourselves in the process."[2]

Let us then plunge ourselves into the process, by turning to the first lines of *FirstDays:*

> *Writing had returned, the stream, the*
> *slender silent stream with its singing*
> *arms, the blood flow in the veins*
> *between the bodies, the wordless*
> *dialogue from blood to blood, with*
> *no sense of the distances, the magic*
> *flux full of silent words flowing from*

one community to the other, from
one life to the other, the strange
legend, inaudible except to the heart
of one or the other, the narrative
weaving itself on high, who will
decipher it, the throbbing weave of
clandestinity,

   Writing, that link, that growth,
that orientation had returned,

   Space is full of voices again, the
whole body is heart.

A return to writing is hereby announced, return to the flow, to the "force faible" that comes and goes,[3] illuminating and animating lives, deaths, moments that persist in the person of the author, in her unconscious, in her dreams, in her breath and blood, very much like the ineffable tide of the sea with its ebbs and flows, coming from the body, giving the life of the body shape and tempo, presenting the past as memory made lyric, and moving, inexorably, toward death.

Not the death we detest: death the teacher, the exhilarating invitation we can only respond to with a complex and resounding *yes.* Indeed, at one point in this text the author tells us she had thought of calling this book *Mes Morts,* which we must translate as both "My Dead" and "My Deaths." The title *Jours de l'an* also resonates with more than one meaning: Days of the Year, New Year's Days, New Year's Days of the Year, or, finally, FirstDays of the Year, a book of days in which every day is newly born, a birth day for the year and for the author.

FirstDays is rife with stops and starts, meanderings, small books collapsed within the larger, leftover object-book we are presented. As in other contemporary texts, what happens in *FirstDays* is the drama of the writing of *FirstDays*, the attempt to write it, wherein the reader is made privy to all the gropings, pantings, hesitations, and doubts, the tensions between the writer's selves and her authorness. The finished product is not a permanence, but proof of the process itself:[4] it is a trace, traced in ash, of a scene of writing that has since gone up in flames.[5] This is especially so in *FirstDays,* in that it is the drama of the writing of the book the author has always resisted, and is still resisting, even while writing. In order to write it, the writer questions the book, wrestles with it, thereby questioning and wrestling with herself, seeking to find and enter the truth of this book she doesn't really "want" to write.

In its turn, the book takes on a life and direction of its own, against and inside all the other books the author permanently carries inside of her. It takes on shape and contours, becomes its own story, even as she, the author, hesitates to tell it. Cixous describes this process, of struggle and confusion with regard to competing identities and desires, as akin to the struggle between the matador and the bull in the arena:

> *One can die from being unable to write in time the book one has in one's body.*
>
> *This is the book that must be braved, it demands of me a courage I desperately seek to call up in myself. I fight against myself. The*

way I fight with myself is akin to the
fight of the matador against the bull.

In the arena, am I the matador
who deep down doesn't dare charge
unreservedly at the bull, who instead
calls him from a ways away, or else
am I the bull who doesn't respond,
who attacks neither the matador nor
the other two people provoking it?
And yet there must be an end—if
there is an arena, there is sure to be
an end—little by little the bull and
I approach each other, and then I end
up hurling myself at the beast, right
at him; he doesn't run away, and
from closer up I can clearly see him
standing on his two hooves, with his
two enormous black horns, known to
all eternity, and finally I charge at
you, matador, and what had to
happen happens: the bull is after all
much stronger than I, even if he
doesn't know what to do. The hand-
to-hand battle is brief! . . . I take him.
So it is. I am victorious without
further struggle. I have him. Then,

to my horror, behold the beast
condemned to death, for this is
the rule of the arena. Don't kill him,
I screamed, for something makes him
me, he's my bull, don't behead him,
I scream, but alas they drag him off
and execute him. There is something
cruel and unjust in this execution.
After all, the struggle wasn't what
you thought, I went too far, and it
was too calm. Without my bull I am
nothing more than a signifier without
a body. The word matador *resounds,*
without echo, in the arena.

In this passage we witness the grapplings of a self struggling with writing itself, attempts to break the petrified nature of received language and render it poetic. In the French, the struggle is most manifest in the moments when pronouns mix and mingle, thereby representing overlapping subjectivities and genres. Replaced by their pronouns *lui* and *il*, the opponents become indistinguishable, interchangeable, just as, later on in the text, the author and her foreignness, her feminine *étrangeté*, fuse in the use of the pronoun *elle*. As translator, I grappled with how to communicate not only the flow and rhythms of this passage, but also the weave of pronouns that produces the startling slippages between the matador and his bull.

From writer Clarice Lispector's Brazilian Portuguese,

Cixous learned a strategy for further complicating her problem—our problem—with pronouns.[6] Portuguese enables us to imagine a subjectless verb, along with all the philosophical ramifications such a syntax implies. In her book *Passionate Fictions: Gender, Narrative, and Violence in Clarice Lispector,* scholar Marta Peixoto criticizes Cixous for making much of this particular Lispectorian usage, which, Peixoto accurately reminds us, is relatively commonplace in Portuguese.[7] Yet isn't one of the gifts of *écriture* to denaturalize, to bring forth and make suddenly, stunningly present, that which usually goes unperceived due to its very, embedded, "naturalness"? Certainly, one reason for learning other languages, for reading other literatures—even in translation—is to benefit from the intriguing, mind-altering experience of discovering how other languages think, how other grammars, other syntaxes, produce and shape thought differently.

For example, consider Cixous's notion of the importance of *le corps*—in English translated and thus read as *the body*—to the act of writing. In her 1991 book *Essentially Speaking,* Diana Fuss comments on the Adrienne Rich essay "Notes Towards a Politics of Location," in which Rich calls for "a moratorium on saying 'the body.'" Fuss judges Rich's distinction between saying "my body" as opposed to "the body" as "a useful place to begin the project of reintroducing biology, the body *as matter,* back into poststructuralist materialist discourse. . . . *The* body connotes the abstract, the categorical, the generic, the scientific, the unlocalizable, the metaphysical; *my* body connotes the particular, the empirical, the local, the self-referential, the immediate, the material."[8] This distinction, however, is less meaningful in a French context, precisely because in French one does not typically use the possessive pronoun to qualify the body or its parts. Thus there is in French an ever-present ambiguity to *le corps;* context determines whether *le corps* connotes the grand, vague, eternal, mythical body or a particular material body in any given instance. Moreover, such contextual distinctions are not necessarily clear, absolute, or permanent.[9] To some important extent, then, the French language itself is constitutive of Cixous's *écriture*.

In short, attempts to read Cixous as a theorist with a stable point to make, especially if one reads her in English where so many of her writing's oscillations and multiplicities of meaning are lost, have failed to recognize the ways in which Cixous's use of the French language is, I believe, a privileged example of differences in perpetual motion—linguistic differences as well as sexual differences. Indeed, perhaps Cixous's poetic playing around with sexual difference has proved perturbing to some precisely because, as a rule, we do not take kindly to being unable to *know*, to being denied the illusion of stable and recognizable categories.[10] Cixous's poetic practice critiques and performatively deconstructs these very categories and must therefore be understood as an attempt "to cause contradictions to vibrate," as exactly the extent to which it cannot be pinned down but remains as movement, and as escape.[11] We might liken her use of language and metaphor to a poetic example of what in chaos theory is called a series of, oxymoronically titled, "unstable fixed points."

Additionally, as we have noted, in French one is exposed to a linguistic system wherein all objects, all concepts, all nouns are gendered. In concert with Calvin Thomas's contention in his book *Male Matters* that "writing can be thought as a scene of gender ambiguity," I am arguing that different languages accommodate this ambiguity to greater or lesser degrees, and in different ways.[12] For example, in writing and reading French, we are invited to visually and linguistically inscribe, refer to, represent, construct, and attempt to grasp gender and its terms. Indeed, it may be worthwhile to investigate, in the context of translation theory, the place and importance of the definite article and its genders for French theoretical as well as poetic vocabularies, particularly as this difference consistently produces a certain amount of static in English translations from the French.

The gendering possibilities within French are especially important for Cixous, who is never unaware when she uses them that the nouns for writing, truth, death, and soul are all feminine in French, whereas the word for book is not. As a reader of Cixous I am forever moved by the insistent presence of the feminine in her writings; as her translator, I am faced with the often impossible task of rendering that feminine into English. How should one carry the gender of thoughts (*la pensée*—there's another one: thought is feminine in French) and objects over into English? As gendered pronouns occur ordinarily in French, perhaps in translation we should not hesitate to let their gender simply drop. But if the commonplace of gendered pronouns is consciously played with, brought to our attention, personified, made central as it is so often in Cixous, what then?

In the following passage from *FirstDays*, Cixous plays with an image of her books as metaphorical male companions:

> *For years I wrote this book, that*
> *book, always joyfully, whichever one*
> *came along, then passed, then the*
> *next one, and while I was writing*
> *I belonged to that book alone,*
> *I thought only of him, there was no*
> *other book in the world than the one*
> *I was pursuing, for as long as we*

traveled together, mysteriously
united, one stretched out on the
other, one emerging from the other's
side, one suckling the other, and
I never wondered who we were for
each other, we were unknown and
carefree.

In response to the dilemma outlined above, I have chosen in this translation to maintain the gender of nouns whenever Cixous chooses to personify these concepts over the course of an entire passage, as seen here. Admittedly, this choice has its limitations: for one, great care must be exercised so as not to overload a passage, thereby rendering it more cumbersome in English than it is in French. For another, bringing forth the multiplicities of meaning does not really solve the theoretical problem, in that it resolves the tensions. It does not maintain the layers, the nonfixity of the many meanings ceaselessly jockeying for resonance and position in French; rather, it emphasizes and makes manifest what in French is only suggested by dint of reading, of actively doing a reading. But as a translator that's exactly what one does: an act of reading; translation is an intensive form of reading; it is a hermeneutical process. My translations inevitably offer *my* readings to the English reader, within certain parameters that, hopefully, have helped me avoid heavy-handedness.

In *FirstDays*, words carry the writing along; wordplay serves as a way of getting on, of moving forward. Writing for Cixous is something one launches, it is "under way," "heading toward"; it is both movement and path. Hence she works words and explores the relationships between them—their similarities of letters or sonority or assonance—by means of the language itself. One of her greatest strengths as a writer has always been her ability to mine, in a quasi-Joycean manner—we would do well to recall that her academic formation was as a Joyce scholar—the French language, teasing out and "uncovering," as Cixous scholar Verena Andermatt Conley has put it, its multiplied meanings, particularly, as we have seen, with regard to gender and its many terms. Finally, therefore, to translate Cixous I often simply surrender to the instinctual; in a word, I have sought to yield to equivalent forms of play in English whenever possible.

A final particularity of Cixous's work I shall focus on here is the extent to and way in which her writing is traversed by others, most often by other poets. Cixous has never "outgrown" the childlike state of immersion and wonder—what Wittgenstein calls "living within the pages of books"—whereby one's reality, one's sense of one's many selves, fictional characters, their authors, times, places, and languages, all coexist in a heady swirl concocted from a brew of identifications, associations, and reflections. Or, as Cixous puts it in *FirstDays:* "Is absolutely unavowable: the passion for books, the ferocity, the need, the exultation, the haste to flee the places inhabited by those close to me, in order to regain the poets and other characters, in their books." She goes on to name the reading experiences she has had with the writings of others' "imaginary memories," which she describes, referring in *FirstDays* to her response to the texts of Paul Celan, as akin to "weeping for what I hadn't had, what I hadn't lost, like a woman suffers from having lost the child she never had, and this suffering, sustained and fed by no body, famishes her infinitely, and deprives her of the stories and the words for soothing suffering."

Thus, just as Cixous hopes that her own "messages in a

bottle" will one day be found and read, so she continues to play her part in receiving and uncorking the messages of her many literary others. She is committed to remaining receptive as a "human heart"—scanning the horizon, waiting by the shore to pluck from the sea the bottle containing the message that will become the poem—to borrow, as Cixous does here, a metaphor from the poet Celan. For example, in *FirstDays* Cixous explains writing's initial absence in the following way: "It was land that was missing, the port, the other shore, and, over there, the unknown house, the sister who might receive the letter and adopt it." In Cixous's universe, such commitment from another—reader or sister poet—is essential to the writing process itself.

This relationship to the other has proved disturbing to some. Most recently, Marta Peixoto, in her previously mentioned book on Clarice Lispector, has criticized Cixous's relationship to Lispector, the twentieth-century Brazilian writer who has been the most prominent among Cixous's author-others for the past two decades. Peixoto reads Cixous's readings of Lispector from the point of view of a Lispector scholar, a perspective that proves, in her provocative book, both fruitful and thought-provoking. Nonetheless, I would like to note my disagreement with Peixoto's conclusion that Cixous's relationship to Lispector is one of appropriation, of erasure of Lispector's otherness. I would argue that the relationship may be more usefully described as that of an accompaniment. For, in addition to finding inspiration in Lispector, Cixous and thus her writing have been transformed by the encounter. Although Cixous initially describes the meeting with Lispector's texts as a discovery—indeed, the date of her first reading of Lispector, October 1, is one of the dates illuminated in *FirstDays*—of a privileged example of *écriture féminine*, to continue to define the rapport in only this limited way is to ignore Cixous's more recent writings, beginning precisely with

FirstDays of the Year. Ultimately, Lispector's *écriture* has served as a springboard for Cixous, especially the 1973 *Agua Viva* (The stream of life), whose translucent, marine economy of the instant is altogether taken up by Cixous in her later texts.[13]

FirstDays echoes *Agua Viva*'s paradoxical temporality of the ephemeral and the infinite: in both texts, the body is inscribed as at once evaporating and, because of that very evaporation, preparing to take its eternal place in the universe as atoms. For example, whereas Lispector dictated her last fragmented writings to a friend when she was literally on her deathbed—fragments that consisted of an evocation of the white lilies that she imagined would soon be found growing from her chest—Cixous writes in *FirstDays* of her own steps toward eternity, in a passage that sheds light on the mystery of one of her most important dates, February 12:

> *Now I am going to tell you why this book's story began* the day after February twelfth.[14]
>
> *Certain dates belong to me: December 9, October 1, July 27, February 12. What is characteristic of our dates is that they return. . . .*
>
> *They bring us: the end of the world. . . . Among them all, the first, the one that unfolded in my forest the footpath of dates, is February twelfth. February twelfth is the arrow that hit in me the beyond . . . and*

*when I will have been atoms for
generations, somewhere at the foot of
an Asian jasmine a February twelfth
will produce a slight quivering of
atoms. Somewhere in the world, me
as memory and pollen, as jasmine, I
will remember and I will make a
white flower bloom. One very distant
February twelfth. But already today
this is known in the universe.*

Interestingly, as we learn from Peixoto, *Agua Viva* is a text that Lispector drastically revised, uneasy about the reception that she, known as a writer of fictional characters and recognizable narratives, might sustain with regard to this raw, liquid, naked presentation of subjectivity, this brand-new—for her—form of "life writing." Lispector's friend the philosopher José Pessanha—that such cautionary criticism comes from a philosopher is not without irony and importance—responded to a draft of *Agua Viva* in a way similar to that in which some readers respond to Cixous: "I tried to place the book: notes? thoughts? autobiographical fragments? I came to the conclusion it is all of that together." Pessanha then wonders what will come next in Lispector's work: "After this meeting of you-Clarice with you-the-writer. . . . Will you continue to be your own theme, a directly presented, naked face without the mask of character?"[15] With the exception of her plays, Cixous has never had much use for the mask of characters; I believe it is in some measure for this reason that her texts have been understood so partially and, more significantly, far too little read.

In closing, I will call Cixous's textual practice, in a reiteration of Paul Claudel, an act of *co-naissance*, a play on the word in French for knowledge, *connaissance*, and its homonym, a word we might translate as "co-birth." The "I" of her text is born, and simultaneously the world is born to her as a way of knowing: knowing as an immediate and reciprocal act. For Cixous, writing, like reading, proceeds by groping in the dark, sensorially seeking to discover some version of some truth about emotions and events, as opposed to being a reporting or linear unfolding of that which has already passed or been surpassed. I will also name this practice an edge pursuit: a pursuit of the edge, practiced on the edge; an edgy pushing at edges in an effort to feel and fall over them. Dreams, too, are edge phenomena, and Cixous follows the flow of writing in a way that is reminiscent of psychoanalytic dreamwork—in search of what constitutes the edge, what functions as the irreducible at the edge. We might further imagine a similarity between Cixous's art and that of a blind sculptor, who amazes by her ability, through touch alone, to produce recognizable portraits of her models in clay.

I have made a point here of acknowledging and naming my personal predilections as a translator in the hopes that, once acknowledged, the whole matter of translation may, in the words of Willis Barnstone, "be forgotten, so that the poem before us can be read as an original act."[16] Nothing is ever received in the same form as it was sent, especially when the flight is a transatlantic one, as Derrida explained years ago in his book *The Post Card*;[17] all readings are generated to some degree by misreadings, mitigated by the instants when "co-naissance" manages, fleetingly, to occur. Translating Cixous has allowed me to live intimately with not only Cixous's language but my own language, the English tongue. This, finally, is what is at stake: a good translator is not to be defined by the extent to which she successfully serves as walking source-language/target-language dictionary. That is what dictionaries are for, and we don't need to duplicate their terrain of usefulness; we need, rather, to consistently avail ourselves of many good ones, which indeed I have done. What makes a good translator, particularly of poetry, is the writerly sensibility one brings to the table in one's own idiom, and the extent to which the sensibilities of the two writers, author and translator, manage to mesh harmoniously. In sum, translation is collaboration; for me, it has been an attempt to give rise to a double art.

I have written elsewhere of the project of translation as transformation, of the inevitable (in some ways sad because of the losses incurred, in others exciting) shifts within a text that come to pass in an attempt to carry it from one language to another.[18] Such a project is in fact a commonplace, in that we as readers and writers of our own lives and of literature are forever translating ourselves through prisms of different and differing genres and genders, forever blurring boundaries between fiction and autobiography, poetry and prose, sexuality and gender, identity and difference. Years ago, Cixous invented a verb in French, *transer,* an act and a state of being. In a transitive sense, it describes the act of moving across, of crossing borders; intransitively, it describes the state of being in motion, being in transition. Make no mistake: we *need* this word and its experience in order to transgress, to transport, and to translate.

I wish to thank the following people for their patient and generous assistance in the preparation of this essay and my translation: Anne Boyman, Louisa Castner, Catherine McGann, Sylvie Romanowski, Marguerite Sandré, Tim Sheie, Ann Smock, and, above all, Hélène Cixous. I would also like to thank participants at the conference Memory, the Body, and Life Writing (organized by the French Department at Northwestern University, September 1995), particularly Nancy K. Miller, Alice Jardine, and Mary Lydon, for their encouragement and support, as well as my new colleagues at the University of Northern Iowa, for their helpful comments on earlier versions of this essay.

FIRSTDAYS OF THE YEAR

Writing had returned, the stream, the slender silent stream with its singing arms, the blood flow in the veins between the bodies, the wordless dialogue from blood to blood, with no sense of the distances, the magic flux full of silent words flowing from one community to the other, from one life to the other, the strange legend, inaudible except to the heart of one or the other, the narrative weaving itself on high, who will decipher it, the throbbing weave of clandestinity,

Writing, that link, that growth, that orientation had returned,

Space is full of voices again, the whole body is heart. It was land that was missing, the port, the other shore, and, over there, the unknown house, the sister who might receive the letter and adopt it.

"It has been thirty years now," . . . *thought the author.* And stopped. "It has been thirty years now," resounded the thought. And the author heard the phrase, and it was the first time. She was, then, today, a person, a woman, who could say: "It has been thirty years now . . ."

So I have a thirty-year-old now. This is what has happened to her on this day already so chock-full of birthdays and anniversaries.

A thirty-year-old now had summed itself up. Suddenly she found herself in possession of thirty years she could fit wholly inside her hands like a book. And it was a book, she thought. A lost book.

Writing had indeed just returned, the promise, the force, the source that knows only pulsation, retreat, return. I'm going to write, she had thought at first, in the comfortable triumph of a boat lifted anew by the arms of the tide.

But I am thirty years old, senses the boat, I weigh thirty years, feeling the enormity of this number for a boat, and the light, limitless power of the tide. Writing is eternal, it knows neither weight nor time. It's going to lift and carry me as it has already thirty times, effortlessly, she thought.

But it was the first time that she, the author, had ever chanced to toss some time in front of the ancient, mysterious event of writing. Human time. Woman's time. Up until now there had been only one year every year, with about two or three seasons. She had lived from present to present, ageless, as one writes.

And all of a sudden, today, the present opens, enter the genius of time, passing through her own chest. And it is she herself who utters this strangely foreign phrase. (A human phrase or rather a woman's, that she would have never said, a mortal's phrase.)

In the exact moment when writing arrives once more and spreads its superhuman élan from one body to the other. She says: behold now thirty years . . . And behold: a whole story arose. Whereas writing doesn't know the story. Arose. Lost story that will not be told. Like a forgotten someone speaking to her. Story that suddenly challenged her destiny.

For the past thirty years, a story had been in the making and she hadn't written it. She hadn't denied it. She hadn't thought of writing it. Her foreign story. So strangely foreign (she thought of it with love, as of someone over there somewhere) one might have wondered if it existed. It was better not to think about it.

And for thirty years I have been writing, borne by writing, this book that book; and now, suddenly, I sense it: among all these books is the book I haven't written; haven't ceased not to write. And it is now I sense it, today, one day after February twelfth I learn this and not before: here is the book I've missed.

To me, this is a blow, a threat.

Now and not before. And once again it is the thirteenth of February, always on this day.

And before that day for years I wrote this book, that book, always joyfully, whichever one came along, then passed, then the next one, and while I was writing I belonged to that book alone, I thought only of him, there was no other book in the world than the one I was pursuing, for as long as we traveled together, mysteriously united, one stretched out on the other, one emerging from the other's side, one suckling the other, and I never wondered who we were for each other, we were unknown and carefree.

See what can happen to us: for thirty years we never think about the book we do not write. There is a book. That we do not write. We barely think about it, almost not at all, almost never; it does not exist. I forget about it. And yet this nameless thing returns, this voice stronger than my voice, but wordless, this voice I obey and I disobey. This . . , this poem, then.

(She had tried to figure out how to call this unwritten book. This object of restraint—this unripened expectation—and, lacking a name for designating a thing that was not of this world, our own, the visible, had proposed to herself the word *poem*. This was not entirely unfitting - : - the distant existence of the book, its starry wandering about which we sense, without ever seeing it, the presence of an order other than our own, so much so that we do not know if it has already taken place or if it will take place in a million years, seemed to her to relate this book to the species of the poem. Poems, too, are of this astral nature, sparks as they are of a dead or distantly imminent fire.

And what this book and a poem had in common was the physical sensation, the cardiac certainty, of their both belonging to a wholly other time from our time to us all. A poem merely passes, coming from elsewhere then moving on. Signifying to us, in passing, at its passage, this elsewhere.

Well, this book was from elsewhere.

An elsewhere that was not irrelevant to her. But in the same way that the unknown game played by the stars among themselves is not irrelevant to us. We are aware of the fact that they are at play, but we will never know what they will have made of our life. What thread they will have gently pulled.)

This . . . "poem" then. This latent book, that had never sketched a step, made a clear sound, see how it seems to expect, intend, solicit recognition from this world? An incarnation?

There has always been this forlorn, far-off song, this music from a native land not found on any map, and that we all believe to be, by definition, lost, that we will never go back to, where we have never even been except one time, the first time and the last.

Just as the author had thought, it was the terrestrial land that was missing, the one we call the "true," the one with passports, where we enter and exit, with professions, big cities, woods of hazelnut trees, what was missing was the singable, edible, detestable land,

---

So how do they exist—this land, this book, this song—lost? In the land of lost lands. In the land where—with words, music, images, with desire and pain—we nonetheless do not have what it takes to make a whole book.

Well, it was this one, the lost one, the lost-safely-stowed-away one, that I seemed to have been thinking of all these years, each time I would read certain poems by Celan, the author thought. To which I would cling, weeping, as if to my own memories.

To my own imaginary memories: weeping for what I hadn't had, what I hadn't lost, like a woman suffers from having lost the child she never had, and this suffering, sustained and fed by no body, famishes her infinitely, and deprives her of the stories and the words for soothing suffering.

Quenching her heart's thirst at the singing pain, *von hinter dem Schmerz,* behind the pain.

Behind the pain, sprouts the poem.

A pain was coming true, something she hadn't known before was stating its name.

Often we suffer from sufferings we've never encountered in this life, never felt while we were alive. And yet they know us and haunt us. Surely, then, we've encountered them in another life (which one? That is a question I call on myself to answer one day, the author tells herself), and surely we need, need to suffer them in this life, the one assigned to us.

In this same way have I always suffered from being blind, from losing my sight, from having eyes that suddenly cloud over from crossings-out, and even though I clearly see this is a metaphor, the pain that strikes my eyes is not a metaphor.

She continued on in this way each year, pestering, greedily, skimming pages, seeking, hoping to find and finally finding,

The poems, this one, and also another, that gave to her the lost tears.

And she found: *Cello-Einsatz.*

Holding the book very close to her chest, she brought the poet's words to her heart's forbidden lips. His words. Eyes closed, reading the music with her heart's eyes, *Cello-Einsatz, von hinter dem Schmerz,* the poem between her breasts, her breasts quench their thirst at the stream of sounds. And taking pleasure from each line she hadn't written. That had to have been written. God had provided, otherwise a pain would have died unsung. Taking pleasure from each pain she hadn't had the chance to feel, but which, fortunately, had been felt—sung. And whose scansion, whose rattle she recognized. For it suffered in her mourning tongue, the cherished, inherited, hated tongue, it suffered from suffering in the adored tongue we can no longer love; the tongue that must be bitten and torn out with our own teeth, and spat, weeping, into the spicy dust.

Her German tongue of German mourning, in which she would never write, which she needed in order to make the tortuous the twisting beauty of pain resound.

At each reading, an unbearable sweetness upon hearing the words she might have moaned in another life—with the two, with the four first accents—would burst into her chest, coming from the source of regrets, Cello-Einsatz, and for the hundredth time as for the first, the sob would rise, rise and with the poem's last accents break upon her heart's rock.

For it will never finish coming true, this poem, this mourning, this sob.

I am like this German tongue, broken, hung, tortured on the wheel, recommencing, she thought, with love for this language, seized, deceived love, love that must deceive and lie to itself so as not to renounce the beloved, I am like this German tongue I keep safely in my mouth, hidden, shown furtively, with a smile that escapes my lips in spite of me. I am like she who attempts to have the cello's carcass rolled into an aviation hangar. Shelter for a broken flight.

This book had been able to exist for years, lost and not regretted, because God had provided for regret. There was Celan. Not only Celan. For years she had distracted and deceived her unrealized passion whose accents were from the beyond, lungs half-asphyxiated with earth and blood.

Celan's gasps (and not only Celan's; Kleist's also, clearer, more warlike—but always in that tongue) had slaked her thirst.

What harm? Just as the cello had been created to moan the animal music of our entrails and the oboe to give wings to the triumphal moods of our adolescences, so a Celan had been created for singing, his mouth full of earth, under the century's cleaver, under the pickax, the only tiny slip of fleshy paper that will succeed in escaping the shovel of the Apocalypse.

I read: "There was nothing more on earth save nothing," Cello said. I read Celan. One tear remained (he said). One tear and no one. The remains of no one. I saw that the earth had become nothing. And there was one tear. Never had there been such a tear. This tear, for me, was the sea.

With a single tear we can weep for the world.

For a while.

And she had wept for several years with one of Celan's tears. A God had provided for her need to weep by inventing Celan, the poet with the name in reverse, the poet who started out being called Ancel, then stopped being called Ancel, then called himself Celan, and thus had emerged from the forgetting into which we had slipped him, *by calling himself contrarily,* and behold him standing on the silent soil, his chest full of cello boughs. Only thus are we able to advance, by beginning at the end, death first, life next, chancy, secret life, so celative, so elative, so celantive, so *celante,*

Mused she, the author, trembling

Sensing it was useless to deny the event.

This nursed life, these years of passion by proxy, from one instant to the next, had just ended.

The book gives her notice: now I await you.

I'm coming, she thought, prostrated. Lying helpless like a woman who has been hit by a car. It is February 13.

The day that began will never end.

In the middle of the day another destiny began. And suddenly we become the hero of a very unknown story. Today is no longer the same today. A yesterday and a tomorrow part with the violence of adversaries. Under the impact we have changed epoch, memory, origin, kinship. We have no more duties, we have no more rights. And we're suffering from a terrible freedom.

What had hit her was the desire to write this book: she wasn't prepared for this, wasn't ready. She didn't recognize herself: so, am I going to desire the undesirable, she wondered?

—What do we desire, if not the undesirable? —No, I myself would have never thought that.

Suddenly her head had filled with unknown complications.

Days and days passed, it seemed to her, without her being able to get up and reset herself to the correct time.

Now she wanted to write this book and she was suffering. She had writing, she had the desire. She hadn't the possibility.

Something in this book was advising her to flee.

She began like this: "The book I want to write, the one I dread writing, is the one that would begin like this: I'm going to tell you at last, and for the first time, everything I now know about the most hidden truth."

With these words, with the word *hidden* followed by the word *truth*, doubt spread out inside her, and just as quickly hopelessness began. She feared. With the one fear, she feared discovering, at the end of a long, cruel excavation, that there was no "hidden truth," that there never had been.

She (truth) was not at the beginning, there was no secret. There were only mistakes and corrections. She feared having to, in the end, lose all hope and all illusion. And those who had always affirmed truth's impossibility would laugh at her.

And at the same time she feared, with the other fear, discovering the truth. And seeing in the end with her own eyes her own face unmasked, to her eternal regret. Yet, she told herself, isn't every discovery true? And everything we say is truth. And we only lie in the hope of creating a more tolerable reality. And lying is often preferable, lying can be a kindness.

Still, Truth had always been her dream. But *reaching* the truth? It seems so far away. The sun hidden behind the sun. Painting Fujiyama. Painters grow on earth so as to paint toward Fujiyama.

The entire history of painting: the dream of painting Fujiyama. But Hokusai's truth: wasn't it—hadn't it turned out to be—that only the impossibility of ever painting Fujiyama authorized the painter to paint and to attempt to paint his entire life? For if it ever came to pass that one succeeded in painting what one had dreamed of painting since the very first paintbrush, everything would perish on the spot: art, nature, the painter, hope, everything would have already come to pass, the mountain would fade into a picture, the picture would lose the trembling desperation that delicately tears at its canvas. A stony completion would seize the universe.

And wasn't the master's truth mad? Didn't his truth have to be that he couldn't paint without hoping not to reach what he hoped to reach? But could one paint in the hope of defeat? It was impossible. The soul of painting lay in the fatal desire to conquer Fujiyama in painting. So the master painted, he dared to make the criminal attempt, counting on death to stop him before the end. Very near to the mountain that filled his dreams. And since he got along well with them (death, the mountain), having lived with them for ninety years, that's what happened.

All the paintings forever breathed this serenity. They were almost perfect. And they no longer suffered from their minimal, quivering imperfection. Not reaching the summit was, in the end, a delicate victory.

Whereas Rembrandt's paintings breathe rage. Disgust for wisdom. The urgent need to seize the sky by its hair, the gods by their feet, to unseal the sun, to drag the whole of nature along in his triumphal procession. The need, at any price, to paint the forbidden. And the truth, if found: he would go so far as to slaughter it in order to contemplate it more truly still. The truth is what he sought, in the depths. "The world is a chest, and I want to paint its living heart," he said. "And in order to paint the world's heart, one must paint with one's own heart equally naked." So that's what he did.

Rembrandt's horrible joy before his canvas, she could see his agony: there he was, painting away like a mad fool, in a silence bursting with all its might, for he was painting with all his might; every nerve ending, every bough, every rib, drawn arched stretched to breaking, his vibrating body unbearable to see, like the awful body of Atlas vibrating under the massive weight, keeping a mad fool's silence about his madness, in a breathless hand-to-hand battle— legs shackled, gripping himself with each brush stroke, wrenching his arm from his arm, his chest crushed by his chest, himself turned against himself, and, in an extenuating effort, ridding himself of his irons, releasing his throat from his own hysterical grasp, and straightening himself up all bloody, skinned, his teeth clenched upon the cry, victorious, having conquered, having wrenched victory from himself—he was painting beyond painting, painting his prey, painting astride a foaming steed, pursuing an army in retreat, with sword blows overtaking and pricking and pinning every escaped detail, and in the end racing over the battle-field that was fast becoming a famous canvas beneath his feet, he burst out laughing, drunk with his own genius. "I conquered Rembrandt," he told his wife, "and I led him to victory."

"One day I'll end up painting astride my own corpse," he murmured at dinner. He ate without appetite, emptied, depressed. Surrounded by difficulties, persecuted, separated from the mirror that was his canvas, he was weak and without genius. The telephone rang. Foreign dealers. He was becoming his reputation. His victories? Esteemed canvases. He sold his canvases. The studio behind the door seemed inaccessible to him. A dream. No one would ever see what he had painted, he thought. Not even himself. He had a cramp in his calf. He was starting to fear sickness and death again, just like before his crises of immortality. The true Rembrandt, he could have wept from it, he never doubted it, was himself.

The lunatic, the one he happened to be sometimes, he couldn't be that one at will. No one would ever know the enormity of his pain. The torment of not being master of his own greatness. Favors were all he deserved. Wasn't he a great painter? The other man, the one he wasn't, the genius, was ferocious, oh marvelously ferocious, arrogant, joyous, he would have thrashed, despised, whipped them, all those admirers who permitted themselves to admire what they were unable to admire, they were incapable, too petty, imitators, and with no idea, not the slightest inkling of the blood he had to shed in order to paint, he would have looked at them and laughed, unmasked them, run them through, and he would have painted them. They who dared to speak of his canvases and weren't afraid to buy them and hang them, as if they were still lives, in their parlors.

But he wasn't that lunatic, not at the moment. At night, eyes open in the dark, lying in his boat, he wondered who, at daybreak, would come to shore. Awaiting, with a dead man's impotence, his resurrection.

If it ever comes about, he thought, I will paint a self-portrait, I will paint all, I will tell all, I will make my secret shine, I will dazzle the whole world with horror. And if I cannot do it directly, from the very first stroke, then I will approach it sideways, I'll start by painting an ox.

It was the ox she couldn't bear. This portrait of the victim painted by the butcher. This (un)pitying self-portrait: one saw in it—without even seeing it—the true Rembrandt, in the incarnadine éclat of his impotence.

She had to close her eyes. It must have taken a mad and foolish courage to paint such a confession. And the ox demanded an equal courage, from whoever contemplated it.

Often in front of Rembrandt she gets discouraged: she doesn't have the courage to look the most powerful part of his art in the face. Just as she cannot look at a blind person without lowering her eyes.

There were books, too, that made her close her eyes after a few pages. Books that look her in the face and tell her exactly what she doesn't want to hear. Nothing bad. Just something that is no one's business. She had respect for these books, and gratitude. It is good that there are books that strike us unbearably. She would have enjoyed reading these books. She would have wanted but not enjoyed reading *The Breath,* a book by Thomas Bernhard she had tried to read several times.

There is charm in disgust. This book knew something about her that she didn't want to know. She would have liked to know what it was. But until now she hadn't made it far enough. There was a secret in this book. Something serious, surely. Hurtful perhaps. A scene? Forgotten? Just barely and with great effort forgotten?

I would have really liked to know what it was. It is through wounds that one enters into a person's secret. The forgetting of a child's death? The forgetting of a child's life? Perhaps? I do not know.

Or else it was a person? One of those people, fortunately rare, whom we have hated, one of those people belonging—we know now, but we didn't know it thirty years ago—to that hated species whose each individual specimen, fortunately rare, immediately provokes in us an explosion of hate, a person we have had the misfortune not to hate immediately thirty years ago because we weren't familiar then with the species, but we hated this person after only a few months' time, and we thought at the time, thirty years ago, that we would never get over it, not that we had committed a crime for him or because of him, but it's just as if we had, we didn't hate him on the spot as we ought to have, we treated him like a person we might have loved, only to realize too late he was the devil—and it is characteristic of the devil to be recognized too late—

we hated hated hated him, despised him, disgraced him, we denied ever having known him, and yet having known him impeded us from living joyfully, we desired his death as the only solution, and by dint of thinking about his death, and of never having known him, we obtained his disappearance, we never saw him again, we never went to hell, we were never in any city where we might have feared being with this person, and we were able, after fifteen years, to be declared cured of the devil.

But thirty years later an altogether similar person can show up, similar in every way, similar forehead, hair, voice, build, who has become the mayor of the little town where we like to spend our holiday, and the worst of it is that the devil hasn't changed at all. We recognize him instantly in a photo; even though it isn't exactly the same person, it's just as if it were. He hurts us just as much as if it were the same. Since he tells us the same thing: that we have fallen upon the person we hate personally, the person made, precisely made for our destruction, fallen upon him as if upon a person we might have loved. Fallen.

Maintaining absolute forgetting is almost impossible but not absolutely impossible. We can succeed at this for many many years. But we must guard against tampering with forgetting, because it is so fragile.

This is why the author, feeling an icy breath rising up from this book called *The Breath*, hadn't persisted until now.

But now, she told herself, hasn't the time come to read the book that raised its fist at me, to look into the face of the person who spit in my ear thirty years ago, hasn't the time come to write the book that maybe is going to slash my chest and my belly, and reawaken my scars, and bring back before me, at night, perched well in sight atop a wooden plinth, a whole row of figurines of all those I had preferred to forget, the book that maybe is going to bite my hands and burn my leg if I don't cross its fiery slopes with a fairly quick and lively step?

—Write the book that's going to strip me? turn me in? What for? she told herself. —Is that what you want?

—I long for truth, I need my truth like a blind lamb needs to nurse, like an ogre needs fresh flesh: like a blind lamb. To satisfy an urgent, blind, primitive hunger. When we hunger like this, we could swallow stones.

If this were true, why delay?

Or else it was one of those paradoxical people we love without knowing whom we love, one of those ninety-year-old children we love without knowing at what age to love them, that we fear loving a little too soon, a little too late—without knowing if a woman can mother a ninety-year-old child. . . .

Or else it is one of those fatal people we love with pure love, purely out of pure love and thus we love them without love, with purified love, because they are fatal. . . .

By dint of hesitating and fearing and delaying, the book grew like an anxiety, one that, if we give it time, ends up occupying the office, the house, the Universe, and engulfing us.

One can die from being unable to write in time the book one has in one's body.

This is the book that must be braved, it demands of me a courage I desperately seek to call up in myself. I fight against myself. The way I fight with myself is akin to the fight of the matador against the bull.

In the arena, am I the matador who deep down doesn't dare charge unreservedly at the bull, who instead calls him from a ways away, or else am I the bull who doesn't respond, who attacks neither the matador nor the other two people provoking it? And yet there must be an end—if there is an arena, there is sure to be an end—little by little the bull and I approach each other, and then I end up hurling myself at the beast, right at him; he doesn't run away, and from closer up I can clearly see him standing on his two hooves, with his two enormous black horns, known to all eternity, and finally I charge at you, matador, and what had to happen happens: the bull is after all much stronger than I, even if he doesn't know what to do. The hand-to-hand battle is brief! Although I am under him, I catch him by the horns. I take him. So it is. I am victorious without further struggle. I have him. Then, to my horror, behold the beast condemned to death, for this is the rule of the arena. Don't kill him, I screamed, for something makes him me, he's my bull, don't behead him, I scream, but alas they drag him off and execute him. There is something cruel and unjust in this execution. After all, the struggle wasn't what you thought, I went too far, and it was too calm. Without my bull I am nothing more than a signifier without a body. The word *matador* resounds, without echo, in the arena.

How could I not be afraid, while writing this book, since I'll have to seize it by its two black horns, of bringing about the death of my bull?

My bull who is myself as well?

There was between the matador and the bull such a mysterious mix of peace and war and resignation.

Nothing is served by struggling in love. One of us must lose her head. Whoever we may be and whatever we may do, in the arena it is written that the beast will die.

Do you want, yes or no, to write this book? I wondered. —How to answer? —Am I not already in the process of writing it? the author wondered.

—I prefer not to know.

This is how strangeness holds me dear, she takes hold of my body, she puts her arms around me, in vain do I think I've managed to distinguish myself, she takes me by the horns, in the very moment I think I've recognized myself.[1] This is what renders so tortuous the desire to write "my" book. I suffer from being unable to separate myself clearly from this strangeness. She worried.

And who am I when writing this book, demi me, demi you, demi dead,

A question that sometimes throws her arms around my neck and hugs and kisses me like a female mosquidog,[2]

Sometimes strangles me with her fingers of string,

for one must, I believe, I believe this, and I would like not to believe it, have an idea or an inkling of oneself in order to be able to begin to write, at least a point, a pivot, a flower root, a beat in the temple, a center of gravity, a sex. Or an other.

One day, wanting to write a book whose character belonged to a world where she herself could never have penetrated, Clarice Lispector couldn't find the way into her own book other than as a certain Rodrigo, a man she ended up becoming at the price of a ticket with no return. She never came back from this book. We cannot kill ourselves twice.

The book wanted it. Her death. It demanded of her an exemplary, unparalleled transgression. How she managed to get to this Rodrigo and yet not get back, I do not know, and I cannot imagine. I might give everything to know, but it would be useless. I am in an oceanography museum, and I am looking a fish in the eye, the one on his left side. The fish resembles a vertical leaf of paper with an eye on each side. The way we look at each other, the fish and I, me

19

held fascinated by incomprehension, he, or she, I don't know, but just the same we look at each other, one eye attracting the other eye like two magnets, and then nose to glass to nose, this is how we look at each other, Rodrigo and I (the look starts with me, it seems to me), two creatures separated by an imperceptible thickness, an untraversable transparency. I can't even talk to him, to Rodrigo, I listen to him, but he renders me mute as though he were constantly lying, like a cassocked priest, whereas I know very well that he only exists beyond the difference between lying and truth, there where a sole light reigns. None of my me's imaginable to me could have written this book, because none could have passed in good faith . . . into the realm of the masculine, to the point of remaining there, high and dry. And to not remain there would have been the sign that it was a simulation, one of those quick-change parts in a play that are intentionally unbelievable. Clarice would never have written a comedy. This book was a tragedy. It is a tragedy. When I read the following lines, "I am not me. I seem to belong to a far-off galaxy, so much am I a stranger to myself," I knew she had really gone off for good to a foreign place, and everything that happened to her from then on would lead her still farther farther from us, as far as that far-off galaxy, where she now makes her home. I saw her go and I wept.

The author that I am can say: I am not me. That's all. I cannot say what Clarice Lispector said as she was leaving. I am not a stranger to myself, not a man. I remain a stranger to myself, and a woman. Ah! if only I could be a man, a foreigner. And then would I write this book with less anguish perhaps? What a deliverance. What an escape (for me). If not, at least a little rest.

But this transgression was a chance that fell to Clarice alone. Even at the risk of death, if I could have, I would have liked to take the same chance, I believe. But it is not mine.

No, I never cease to belong to this world where women's bodies collide. In vain do I meet myself as an old woman, even in my oldest old age, to the point of not recognizing myself and thinking it is my grandmother who is in my bed, it's no use, I am always of this world.

The pain of being so unknown, suffering that drives me mad when a book is struggling with me, it is I who suffers this suffering. She is mine. She is I.[3]

In the masculine I do not know, I do not live.

As bull and matador I am condemned to death.

How am I me? By beginning. By dreaming. By wanting to write. It is a woman who wants to write this book. Not without men. But a woman. The person who is perhaps already writing, perhaps isn't writing, this book, the author of all difficulties, the author of desire, is, I can assure you (more or less), a woman, a little less and a little more.

Could a man have ever known this state of pride that slightly swells the author's body, this heaviness of the heart? I am brooding, I am big with child, I am a little more than myself. I am pregnant with intimacy. I am also something other than the friend who is speaking to you. I stifle a cluck. I take the women by the waist, my future and former sisters. The earth turns, and it is done. Now night falls. Comes the moment for giving birth. Time for the ritual. All is dark. In the foreign room, O what a moment for strange joy. I wait. I surrender myself without any prejudice to the innocence of the event. Never have I been so foreign. Life presents me with one instant after the other and every instant is a surprise. I am immersed in the energetic obscurity of my destiny. A destiny that comes to me today like a never-received telegram. We don't give birth twice in the same stream. This doesn't resemble anything I have ever lived. I am primitive, confident. At last, the child. (How did she give birth? It was a strange joy: that is all a woman can say with words. The essential is strange.) At last, the child.

Where? There. There? There. They have pinned it for me, prudently, to a slip of paper. Of course, the child I have just given birth to is a little small, that's the surprise. It is a twinkling. This tiny scrap, no bigger than a fingernail, pinned to a pretty slip of paper. I'm not sure I approve of the pin. And the tininess? Not to worry. A living child fattens quickly. Once the surprise has passed, nature guides us. Haven't I milk, am I not a nutritious woman? For this, yes. See my breast all black and swollen. From my goat's breast, from my dark black, lustrous breast, made of smooth leather except for a few tiny hairs around the nipple, which I squeeze with the ancient, familiar gesture, willingly drip a few tears of colostrum. You see my body, it, is ready. As for the fact that for the occasion I have breasts as black as coal—you will find the explanation for this in my book.

What matters is that the child sucks, takes, fattens, fills out. I place the child on my dripping breast. "The child." It is here that my troubles begin. The child doesn't suck. I can't believe it. (The author is familiar with this, but not the woman.) I insist. I press the child. No movement. Is there even a mouth on such a small being? A violent, premature question that mustn't be posed. I call for help. Now into the room come women of profession and of generation. Me, trembling, they, lying in my bed, like grandmothers. Anguish begins, with the confusion. It is anguish that, at the worst moments, inspires in us our slips of the tongue and of the pen. I do not know how the child placed on the bed on its piece of paper was awkwardly covered over by the folds of the sheet and by the sheets of paper. "That's all I need," I say to myself; I quickly disengage it. Death by suffocation, I wouldn't be able to get over it, I would never be able to accept it. I press the future child to my chest, its weakness to my strength. And all day long, with all my might, I deny, and I affirm, I deny and I affirm, I switch on and I deny, until daylight's last second I rise up against the night. I who am unfamiliar with death, I who come from grand, durable mothers. But at the end of the day, I will have to return to reality: nothing will have taken, little by little the certainty imposes itself, yes, my body is swollen with futureness, yes, from my black breasts oozes future milk, but this child is really too far from a state of possibility. It's not happening, it's not happening. Mourning seizes me. And overtakes the universe.

What will I say, I wonder, to these women whose waists I held? I will say that I gave birth to a child who died as soon as it was born. But that isn't true. It wasn't a child. It was merely a fragment of incarnate matter, a prehuman fragment, pinned to a slip of paper.

To be a mother before ever having a child, to have the power, the milk, the welling up of writing, and no more nursling than a slip of paper: this is the kind of unprecedented misfortune that can only happen to such a person. Could a man have had this dream?

It is a woman who enjoys and suffers from such preliminary maternity. It takes very little, it must be said, an almost nothing, and her whole body becomes a garden. A line by Celan. Or this morning in the hour before humanity, when all the pine trees' fingers, immersed in the milk of twilight, attempt to pin the sky, before daybreak: the race of two premature squirrels. Behold two beings who know neither high nor low, I observe. Verticality is their leaf of paper, and all is well for her and for her him. To be two free squirrels! To write the book without high, without low, with for earth the sky and for sky the earth. I wish for this.

I will say: I gave birth to a child as big as a child, and it died immediately. A dead child is a child. I will not say: I gave birth to a slip of living paper, as big as a butterfly. That's impossible.

—Impossible? I say to myself. Why?

—I would be accused. I don't know of what. Of the mother or of the child. Of too much, of too little, I don't know.

Such events cannot be said. I sensed this right away.

We sense what mustn't be said, we see the danger coming, and immediately we go to ground. Lying is our animal instinct.

—Shame? Fear that someone will see your black teats, your goat's teats?

—Worse. My black teats are nothing to worry about, next to what I'm hiding.

The Main Character of This Book Is . . .

But after all, why not say it!? (I say to myself. Say what is already being said in me, clearly, unequivocally, say what had a name, and—had this been possible—would have had a body and a face,

the face I almost see, so much do I desire to see it so much do I peer and frown and peer down to the bottom as I have for such a long time; one day I will see it and surely earlier than I'd hoped—earlier—)

why not say it, out loud, and facing it, yes, facing the naked faces (I said to myself; I had gotten to the point of referring to myself as you, of pushing myself, and then gripping myself—clenching up just behind my teeth—keeping myself back, pushing myself forward and going so far as to grit my teeth, to the point of hurting my ears)

and I was the living example of a terror stronger than everything, no, the word *terror* is inexact, it was a panic that I disapproved of and that clung to the roof of my mouth, to my webs and to my walls,

—and you are here, I said to myself, almost overcome from not saying, and by the same token almost beside yourself in the effort to say, to pronounce, to announce what you well know—what you've known obscurely for months already, and clearly now for days—and as if I had myself invented hands for strangling myself and arms for clasping myself and for crushing my own arms, I broke myself, I was broken, bent, nephritic, sometimes seated with my forehead on the table strewn with more and more leaves of paper on which I had attempted and just as quickly missed an exit, and thus

ravaged from the inside from the outside by myself, I bent beneath the assault I made on myself,

—and there is nothing more desperate than this kind of attack, against which we do not manage to defend ourselves, since by defending ourselves we merely double our attack—

—so much so that when I managed to write, after five days of gripping struggle, half a page torn from my own refusal, and when dread's embrace seemed to weaken, from weariness perhaps, and I advanced across the paper like a six-legged spider, I was going to say, I was going to say, writing really seemed to have thread its way through the very tight mesh of my system of terror, and I bid blindly, passively on her,[1] my liberty, I thought I saw the line, the second, when I would say, and of course as soon as the word was uttered, the evil spell tormenting me would instantly come undone,

and since I already saw myself approaching ahead of myself a gate of sturdy bars hewn to spears

terror suddenly manifested itself in my legs, clamped my toes in tongs, and drew my entire conscience toward my feet, which suddenly took on, by right of extreme pain, more importance than my suffocating chest or my head with its eyes scratched out, crossed out, fogged up by the invisible but blinding dust that is stirred up by thoughts struggling against themselves—

—But, after all, why not say it? (I say to myself, and everything would come untied, the anguish undone, and I evoked and almost took pleasure just in evoking the marvelous relief, the loving comfort of rest, the smile, after the extreme effort, after the brushed-against-lived-avoided accident, after the triumphant orgasm) —But a blaze cannot be reasoned with, and I couldn't do otherwise than to let myself be half devoured. And why didn't I say out loud what I distinctly named in my heart of hearts, this presence that accompanies me, this exceptional, enthralling person, this limitless and yet limited and limitable power—this hero and this heroine—I am the one who refers to her thus, but this person is totally deprived of pretension—it is I who humble or exalt her—and for me, perhaps, by the way, because she has shone in me so powerfully for such a long time, that she has therefore become my guest, my secret, my treasure, and because I was far from being displeased— she was in any case and she is an extraordinary being —And even a being I couldn't do without—without whom the world would have no taste, without whose existence the beings I love most in the world would leave me neither hot nor cold (I can say this without fear and without offense, for in any case she is here, there is no risk of her disappearing, so I can imagine the worst without being afraid it will occur)

———————

yes, why then, since discussing this with myself it appears clearer and clearer to me that not only am I not repulsed by this person, even if she is the cause of so many complicated fears, moreover I am not unhappy—and am even, doubtless, happy to feel her in me—and I notice that by saying this I calm myself, I make peace with me, I put a damper on my assaults—

—not only do I feel neither shame nor horror, but in a way, I am very fond of her, I feel affection for her, an attachment—

Ah! now that's said and it does me good. Nothing frets and harms the soul more than to be unable to declare an important attachment publicly. An affection, by definition, wants to proclaim itself. For it is always before the world, in the eyes of humanity, that we love. Love—wants witnesses: feeds on witnesses. Which shows us that we love each other in view of others, and not without staging a scene. Others are our indispensable partners. We love in two's: we who make up the couple—and the others.

I come back to my avowal: I've said it, I feel affection for *her*, next I might qualify this affection, perhaps go as far as to call it a penchant. And I'll go that far at one time or another.

But I am quite conscious of the fact that I was able to make this very necessary gesture of avowal because I had not yet named, declared the object of so many pains.

Why? I avow I fear people's reaction. Fearing is my affair and my fault.

I imagine saying: this character is . . .

And I imagine the reaction: it's as though I were an aging father, so worn out that I've surpassed the era of paternity long ago. I've arrived at that desperate, despairing age when one feels closer to solitude than to any human being. There, where no one succeeds in reaching. And yet I have a child, we always still have children even when we no longer feel like parents, we have pushed beyond the parental stage, and we belong from then on to the other age, the one that none imagines before having gotten there. But this doesn't keep the children from existing and, not suspecting a thing, from pursuing what is for them, naturally, always alive and substantial. So they address themselves to the dead trunk that is us, as if we were still filled with sap, and they don't stop talking to us. And as long as we still have the patience to pretend—which is our duty in relation to those who cannot know that this deparentization happens to parents—we imitate what we once were, we say our lines, thus giving hope, curiosity, and ignorance their cue.

But one day we are too sad and too alone to play along. And then, all of a sudden, we tell the truth about our state. Not much is called for, a few words, but come from our icy cave. Suddenly we say to the child sitting affectionately next to us, trustingly touching our arm: "Leave me alone." What violence! The breath of truth that emerges from our cave grazes the hot face like a cannonball. All of a sudden we didn't play along. The child receives the skeleton's seagull cry, this harsh, furious cry, full in the face, and he shudders, his eyelids quiver, what has just struck him is unnameable, it is foreign, it is so enraged, but with a goalless, hopeless, wandering rage, and look: it has just struck the child without meaning to. The child doesn't understand, but what does *understand* mean, he receives, he winces, he bows, he is warned, he blinks but doesn't see a thing, his roots are laid bare, and he withdraws without saying a word, instinctively he performs the remoteness, the gulf, the farewell he has received full in the face. This is how we fall sad as we fall sick. We fall into the sickness of sadness.

But in truth I imagined even worse, because I am not an aging worn-out father; it had seemed to me for months now that it was bad to be inhabited by this person—and I had gotten to the point of hiding her—and even more so since I am who I am, a woman and on top of that an author, or else an author and on top of that a woman

it seemed to me, I say to myself, I answered myself—although I'd been tempted for a rather long time to simply say who this character is—but as the temptation became more and more insistent, my resistance grew to the point of becoming brutal—that this would be poorly viewed, poorly received. Saying would incite the sentiments I so fear in others—antipathy, distrust mixed with attempts at derision, incredulity—everything that causes others, my brothers, to be my enemies and me to hate them and yet to my constitutional misfortune, I can no more distinguish myself from them than my fingers from my hand. They who are you. It is you I feared, my enemies, you who are me, you of whom I am a part. And from whom I distinguish myself always with hesitation, for if I feel myself to be different, I never know exactly if my difference is mine or if it's yours.

This is how in my fight against myself, one of the women, one of the fighters who is also me, fights me for you and in your name. And to think I might be mistaken. Maybe you're exactly like me? Inhabited, like me, by the same power? Maybe all the fears that have twisted my arm are entirely in vain? Signs of only me. Maybe it is I, alone without you, who have such a prohibition on my tie to this person?

But why make such a production of all this? I say to myself, now, whereas you may very well end up saying it, at least I hope so. Why delay and delay again? Which is, by the way, I know it only too well, a bad way to begin a book.

And why do I delay? As one hopes to delay an execution. Because I think that once said, something will have ended, something will begin. To say it is—I guess—to put an end to it. To what? To a story, mine, and not only mine. At least to an illusion, to speeches, images, beliefs. I fear the end of me, of course, the end that nonetheless has surely already arrived, except we don't know much about it yet. The end of a woman, the one who is still me, who I believe I've been.

Ending doesn't frighten me. No. But don't we tremble from not knowing who else we'll be? We have loved ourselves for dozens of years; now comes the time to learn more about ourselves more closely, in another light. And what would happen if we loved ourselves less? less easily?

And yet at the idea of making another acquaintance, we tremble with emotion.

And already I rejoice at having learned what we only learn by dint of having years to live through: time, our painter, is slow. It takes him twenty years to assemble a portrait that will be our result. After which we resemble ourselves for another ten years, twenty years, while time pursues his work of art, noting and retaining our elements in transformation, until we come to know the person we have ended up being, and everything has changed.[2] And everything will change again. The person we have been is now an "I was," the character from our past. She follows us, but at a distance. And sometimes she can even become a character in one of our books.

This is how I have behind me, one, two, three, four deceased women (and maybe others whose bones and dust are all that's left), of whom one is a mummy, and one could be my friend. The other two I hate.

Left today is the one who will have followed us here. And who passes with me into the present. We cherish this one, the one who has traversed the decades where others fell: she cannot be, we believe, but the strongest and best of ourselves. This is but a belief. Maybe she's the one who in the end will have been us, we think furtively, is it she we will have been? But maybe things will be altogether to the contrary. She will succumb, and all we will feel for her is a distant wonder?

This is how, every fifteen or twenty years, we lose a life and we welcome another. Behold: we are our own oriental bride. And we desire ourselves in fear.

Certain of our familiars know my future before I do. In our own eyes we are, at the age of sixty, still baby chicks in the limestone. I will reveal myself in my own time. My already tenuous shell will burst into bits. I sense that this birth is imminent. Already a part of me is future: everything I've just thought is what I'm going to think in the next hour.

I expect this unveiling like a blow. That I cannot not

strike at myself. My arm is already raised. My neck is already lowered. Suddenly it is very dark inside me (will I be extinguished?).

It is raining hard outside. The squirrels, who know neither good nor evil, yelp like Indians. The house is the same.

Inside me blows a blade's cutting breath.

(What am I talking about, wonders the author? The diary—of a foreboding?)

(Will you believe me if I say: I already know what I'll discover. But at the same time, I don't know. I am on the verge, between already and not yet. My ignorance is pure. I swear it. Do you believe me?)

(What I have been doing these last few instants—for I sense these are the last—is very difficult: I am trying to note *the passage*—I am in the process of passing.)

It is dark here, in this passage. Is she passing on my right? Is she passing on my left?

(And afterward they will say you are obscure. Obscure? Obviously. How could the author not be so: just before the revelation?) (But afterward all will be clear.)

In my obscurity, I am a criminal. The secret is my crime. Having a secret is our crime.

I silence myself: I kill myself. I kill the day, too.

But I shall break the silence. And kill otherwise.

Watch out, because the hour is going to sound. In three lines. I collect myself one last time. As before a separation. Now I am going to open the door. Now I am going to turn on the light. And you will see. I turn it on:

Well, yes, it is death. This presence inside me that didn't want and that hindered me and sat on my heart like a bird of stone trying to hatch a stone. The character I've been greeting for weeks as one greets death, strangerly, backward, blindly, I call her: death.

My death. Which is thy death. Your death, which is my death. This is the main character in what will be this book if it lives.

It isn't what you thought?

I was afraid of this: that I announce: death is my character (and much more besides) and that you would suddenly feel antipathy, anger even. If that's the case, I beg your pardon. And maybe this book won't be what you fear.

I was also afraid of this: that I announce death, after not having spared the suspense, but without doing it on purpose, because death's approach puts the author in a state of quasi hypnosis. Did you know that? You knew it. I beg your pardon. But I don't think you already knew everything about this person.

Death is not what we think. Often she is alive, whereas we, we only think of her as dead. We want death to be dead. And we're not fond of her. Whereas I, I've said I'm not without a certain fondness for her. And if I'm fond of her, others are probably fond of her, too.

Thinking Is Not What We Think

Death is not what we think.

Thinking is not what we think.

Our thoughts are strangers. They come to us in whimsical shapes that resemble them. We do not recognize them. Because during our story's most interesting circumstances, we do not recognize ourselves. Living is: advancing straight toward the unknown to the point of getting lost.

At the risk of losing ourselves. It takes risk.

(At least for an author. An author is a person to whom life happens in unknown chapters. Life whose author is not the author. My story has as its authors the characters I love and who call to me. This is why I never know what I'll be doing next year.)

Have I ever thought at the calm pace of my thought? Have I ever taken a path and followed this path familiarly to the end, either on foot, or by car, have I ever reached the goal I was aspiring to when I started on my way? I have no memory of this.

Whenever I would reach a place, a country, a house, the sea, a room for love, a freedom stretched out before the iron gate, it was never the goal I thought I had aimed for, it was always the other.

Thinking is not what we think.

We try to believe we can think sitting in an office, in a car, in a plane, with us in the cockpit, our hands on the steering wheel, the steering wheel in our hands,

but it's not like that at all, not at all,

thoughts arrive unleashed, impassioned, from all over, under all shapes and forms, and as we do not have enough strength, energy, electricity, clues, hands, seconds, to receive them, they pounce on us, stone, bombard, daze, transport, fleece us—us, puny seeds, mere ninny grains, intelligent but minuscule—in a dazzling tempest, and with our fingers with our lips our eyelids, greedy tortured, we try to catch hold of all we can; we cling frenetically to the flaps, the folds, the fringes of these genial giants.

The tempest passes. We are run aground, swirled around, having wrested a few atoms from the wind, and that's already immense. And yet it was *I* who unleashed it. I press a button and lo, the world's explained, but all *I* command is the button. To think? To founder. To founder: to think.

Author, have you ever written the book you wanted to write? What is an author? wonders the author. The shipwrecked, the vanquished survivor of a thousand books.

I had only not to want? That's impossible. We want. That's always how it starts. I wanted. I bore the brunt of a thousand tempests and saved some thirty shells.

Have I ever wanted to write a book and believed I was writing it? I've tried. In the end a book is left. And I adopt it.

———————

Have I ever lived a book page by page?

I'm present at takeoff. Yes, it is *I,* it is *my* body that, most of the time, takes the first step. But not always. It is really us, this powerful ensemble that we constitute when we—my blood, my body, my writing, my goal—are duly assembled, and the author that we are isn't missing a thing, not a breath, not a nerve ending, not an article of clothing, starting with our socks.

In these cases, I rejoice. We run belly to the ground through the night to bring the message. For it is at night that we run to carry the message, never during the day. That is why I rejoice (not from pride, but from boldness). The feeling of power is so very pure: it is the mission, it is the message that create the power. What we carry likewise carries us. Belly to the ground, the road is long. It is spinach green and unfolds at length its long, dark-green strip beneath our belly, belly to the ground. We run, never stopping, covering kilometer after kilometer our head barely raised, surveying the distance kilometer after kilometer as far as the horizon, the night is dark, the road narrow, we run along it at a rapid, regular rhythm, belly to the ground, head raised, hoping unsuccessfully for a sign of light, here and there at a distance in a foreign land, feeble phrases light up in the night, candles that only illuminate the length of the road and the dark space to be covered; nonetheless we pursue without getting discouraged, knowing that the essential is to continue, until brusquely I reach, without transition, what awaits me: the Impassable Stairway.

It is always the same repellent Stairway, the rising stairway, the stairway that presents every difficulty, we have to climb it like an insect, with our back wavering over the void—for the front of the stairway is concealed from us, we must crawl up it from behind, each movement takes an hour, a thick, heavy hour—and extract each gesture from the worldwide stillness, liquid granite, thick as chocolate hardening, in the crushing pain of the mire. And so we go along, suffering. Until the bend. For the stairway leads to a bend. The earth, the destination, are on the other side of the wall, above the stairway, to the north. And how to reach the North floor from the South without an inconceivable reptation? How to reach the beyond from beneath? And from within to discover the without? One must turn the moon upside down, walk on one's own head. Reality is so close, nonetheless it is inaccessible. The verso wants to extend over to the recto. How will tails become heads?

Life on many stories is an author's fatality, we submit to it and we cannot give it up. Would I give up my blood, my bone structure, my wavering back, the opposing stories that are my heritage, the worldwide mire I cannot not struggle against without getting discouraged, and the feverish hope that one day I will find the passage, the way in. And then there will no longer be between the living and the dead this page of stone and earth that separates us. Between us the living and us the dead.

———————

—You want to write the book of the dead? —This is the author's awful hope.

And the message? Ah, the message. We would only have known it on arrival. Surely it is the truth. What pushes us to run thus, belly to the ground to the end of the spinach-green road and to the limit of our human strengths, can only be: the greedy, powerful need that knows no distraction, to cleave the chests, to open all the cupboards, to read aloud all the love letters and all the telegrams . . .

And what holds us back all of a sudden as hard as it pushes us is she also, is her proximity, it is she who at the same time attracts us, calls us, causes sources of superhuman energy to explode inside us and from one instant to the other, in the very moment when we're about to reach her, reduces us to nothingness. But it is obviously because she is so close that this catastrophe occurs. And since we guess as much, in our pain, in the evening at the way station, bruised all over as we are, and so far from our point of departure that there is no question of turning back, our heart crushed, our thigh and back muscles pinched like the strings of a mourning lyre, we cannot dream of simply turning around.

Sometimes, even the departure escapes me. I'm not ready. I spend my time misplacing the minuscule message stuck to a butterflyer among the dozens of articles of clothing I've strewn about. Everything I touch, I lose, I sow dispersion all over the plain. Distraction reigns, seconds fall from time, nothing holds and I hold on to nothing. The earth's surface is in the state of before God, I don't possess the secret of Genesis. Nature without order. I am, too. Then comes the car, without explanation. The car I climb into takes off so I'll notice that I'm in back and not in front, that nonetheless it's moving, more or less following the steep road's curves, but because chance is still more or less driving it, I try to make my body one with it, to imprint a correct movement onto it with the tension in my muscles, I try to stop it in order to move to the front to the steering wheel, but how to stop it when cars are passing on all sides, not a stretch of propitious sidewalk, and so we descend like a fish in distress, miraculously still skillful and propelled by instinct, but promised to destruction if I don't end up taking back the controls. But for the moment it is still the time of the fish, equivocal time, ephemeral era; so the car heads downstream, like a text that has taken off, with no one in front and the author in the backseat by mistake; by mistake: by definition.

My Wombs Tombs

Now I am going to tell you why this book's story began *the day after February twelfth*.

Certain dates belong to me: December 9, October 1, July 27, February 12. What is characteristic of our dates is that they return. On their own sometimes and from afar, from Russia, from Austria, from Algeria, coming from the shore of one country and returning to the shore of another country, they strike me in full peal, with the sounds of Easter and tocsins. And what news!

They bring us: the end of the world. And another end. And another end. And the end of an end. Among them all, the first, the one that unfolded in my forest the footpath of dates, is February twelfth. February twelfth is the arrow that hit in me the beyond, and reddened it twelve times and clawed at the cells of my memory, and when I will have been atoms for generations, somewhere at the foot of an Asian jasmine a February twelfth will produce a slight quivering of atoms. Somewhere in the world, me as memory and pollen, as jasmine, I will remember and I will make: a white flower bloom. One very distant February twelfth. But already today this is known in the universe. The author met an unknown woman in India. The author unknown the woman unknown. The Indian woman suddenly said to her in a lightning flash of affection: You, you were born on February twelfth. Grazed, she said: no, no. Struck. Not at all, she said. The arrow faded. "Then," struck the unknown woman, throwing her next bolt of lightning, "you were born on June fifth." Yes, said the author, standing, struck by the bolt beyond all comprehension. Two clouds of fire breathed the breath of the inexplicable over the open book of her cradle. The author felt herself written, struck with writing. Thus, already in India, the date was in the air. But when this comes to pass in India where we know no one and will never return, it remains in India, we forget that we are the subjects of mysteries, descendants of known or unknown dates, frail seeds of memory that have been lifted and carried up to our prenatal heads, we forget. The author forgets, I remember.

When I enter again as I'm doing today, July fifteenth, as the author enters writing—by the milk-painted door—I enter called by the ancestral calling, the one I have always answered: yes, I'm coming, the imperative, absolute calling that doesn't even need to say my name in order for the nameless soul in me, the aspiring animal, the principle, to feel the sensual, superincarnated pressure that *makes me* do what I do, eyes closed, lips closed: the oath, the renewing of the oath, the alliance with ancestral desire, I enter today, I have entered, I am in the country without exteriority, earth with gardens, country of my people, and I am here because it is the night before and the day after the imperative signal. When the date arrives, time obeys it. If I wasn't born on February twelfth, then I was born on June fifth, which is its synonym. June fifth was my first February twelfth; I learned this later.

———————

Who can say what comes to me on February twelfth? Perhaps a June fifth comes to me one February twelfth.

Today, says my mother, is your father's birthday. Yes, it is his birthday. My father in the red-rock cradle. And now it is my cradle every year, it is my birthday.

On February twelfth came—to me—what only comes once and to one person on earth that day, to me to whom no other date had ever come, no arrow, not one,

February twelfth, 1948, on this date I was broken in twelve, the world exploded like a single soldier on a mine, it was torn to shreds, the world in which I had been conceived and had believed I would dwell. I exploded, and I saw everything. I saw the whole world, it sizzled before me like an enormous fly caught between teeth of flames.

And I was made heroine of the apocalypse. I was consecrated. I wanted to tell you this, but in this very instant I realize I can't: I am inside, I see nothing, around eleven o'clock on the morning of the twelfth, I fall like a stone into an incandescent crater. I remember the hours from before, hours of childhood drawing to a close. The bus was my transportation to the end, it would carry me, the path would climb. The signs seemed to still belong to the familiar book. The familiar K, a letter as familiar as a tamed lion, the *Chemin des Crêtes*,[1] O familiar, familiar, perfectly familiar, the slashed *K* and the road would drive me from stop to stop O excessively familiar the climb to the end, me astride a donkey, me surrounded by silences inside the familiar bus, me enveloped in nothing, surrounded by nothing, escorted by nothing, feeling the weight of no sign, feeling the weight, me with a wild beast dancing and growling in the middle of the path before my heart and seeming not to see it, me scorning the beast, the unknown, strangely unknown beast, not letting any being see what I assuredly did not see, astride my donkey, acting as if, from stop to stop, the path that leads us to the impossible is like this, crawling on all fours with a regular, familiar rhythm, toward the execution. The countryside is a lie: exactly the same as yesterday.

Outside: no difference. None around. All the difference emanating from the faces, emanating from the walls, emanating from the clouds, all the difference, in me, only in me. A difference had crept in. And what a subject she was trying to broach with me. I didn't listen to her. I didn't hear what she was telling me. The alteration rusting my nerves as fast as acid: I didn't notice it. We sense the attack coming, and we oppose it with an icy incredulity; this is our tactic: we warn ourselves and we take no account of the warning, we don't believe ourselves, this is our only chance, we believe, to discourage the sickness. I didn't believe. I manifested a wily, superhuman indifference. I concealed even to myself what I didn't want to see coming. Besides, I didn't see a thing. I didn't hear a thing. I didn't receive the letter. I didn't accept a thing. The prophecy: I said no. Don't you see that this K is not your bus? I said no. The black horses caparisoned in black? No. This cloud stuck above the mountain's crest? I said no. One has never seen a more ferocious, more inconsistent fight. No witness, not even myself. I denied everything, each thought, each person, each countenance, the tinkling of each word, one after the other, I denied; by dint of denying, I escaped. I escaped from them—from them and from me.

I no longer know at which stop, I suddenly knew I was no longer me, hadn't been for some time already. I had gone to such depths. And there below, in the cellar, in the shelter, beneath my earth, I buried something. I don't know what. What I knew? My soul? What I had just invented, this strangeness, this sickness, this replacement, this unsuspected, stubborn me, I buried myself in my own depths, like one buries a corpse, with the same exultant anxiety. But this was not a corpse. It was my ruse. One of my schemes. Quick, without deliberating, the sooner done the sooner forgotten.

The child who gets off the bus knows nothing, the

child of childhood, born to hope and to trust. The execution took place immediately, the front gate barely crossed. A brutal execution. A butchery. What's the use of giving the lamb time to imagine. Eleven o'clock! Time for meat. And no transition. Everywhere, starting at the front gate, all the way to the house, on the tree-lined drive, all the way to the bedroom, and with a single blow to the skull and to the earthly globe. Economy of the slaughterhouse. We don't know how to give death. We kill.

After that my family was a little relieved. The worst for my aunts had been waiting at the front gate, with the knife frightening them in advance.

I, too, I screamed, I screamed, just from seeing what they were hiding from me at the front gate. I frightened them. I screamed, I screamed. And one instant later I fell, I had fallen, through the front gate of this world into the other. From one instant to the other I was no longer of this world. I ran, I was nowhere, I was running, I was fleeing February twelfth, I was fleeing this day's monstrous demand. We are not yet ten years old, and we are asked to swallow the earthly ox in one day, we are asked to tour the birthplace's corpse, and to stop the rivers' flowing, the pine trees' growing, with one stroke of the knife, and to roll the planet into a hole hollowed out in the middle of a field.

And the future, axed, all that I should have done with my father for forty years, axed, all those years.

To swallow a pyramid of bodies in one day, all that has been killed, all that is dead, and to kill all that has not yet died. And me, child of the apocalypse.

The event is too big for the child, careful, the child is going to explode, the child is going to become as confused, enormous, as nauseating as death. Is going to become February twelfth, the madness of this day, her madness.

For it is really her, the child of childhood, that Destruction aims for. We were playing in the playground.

And behold: the Big Cannon—with its muzzle eye—points itself at the little girl. She lifts her head and sees the muzzle of the enormous eye. And it shoots the earthly globe, its eye, at her, it shoots its eye at such a small child.

Only the night before, I had peed in my pants in the playground. And now, a crown of hooks on my head, and my head filled with second thoughts, I reigned over my compatriots the butchered hens, the slaughtered oxen.

We change species, kinship. We belong to the family of orphans and prophets, we know a lot, and we hide it under our age.

(But we unearthed the buried thing on the morning of February twelfth.)

In order to stay in school we play the defenseless child of childhood.

Whereas in truth we are the demon, the goat, the woman on the pyre, the orphans' revolt, the widow's warrior, we have drunk, we have eaten.

We know the taste of rage and hate. I saw you! Allow me to love you no longer, known God, cross-eyed God. I saw your hate, I saw your foolishness, despite your immensity, I am your enemy, I depose you, despite your immensity, God who has dismantled me, I resist you, cross-eyed and uncrowned God.

Size reduced, encircled, backed into a corner in front of the entrance to the school, looked at between the eyes, accused of having lost my father, as if I had lost my hair, my eyes, my teeth, accused by the cross-eyed schoolgirls. As if it were I who was cross-eyed, I who had lost the sword, the right, the crown. They who were cross-eyed, who hadn't lost or tasted a thing, who had never been any larger than themselves, they who had never been murdered, couldn't even imagine, who knew nothing, spoke no foreign tongue, had never imagined or guessed, or sensed, or believed, that there is another world, open, right here behind my shoulder, under the sheet, in the book, they, daughters of merchants and veterinarians, who felt horror and disgust for my freedom.

Everything was backward, and me in the middle of this backward, pinned precisely in the middle of this backward and watched,

I who had seen the end of the world,

For one year, I remained pinned in the middle of backward, encircled, watched, in the world of the daughters of merchants and veterinarians.

I played the fool, I played the child, I didn't tell the truth, I was afraid, I didn't dare proclaim my kingdom, my strength and my grandeur were too small, I remained where I no longer lived.

What stopped me from moving was my lack of citizenship. On both sides. I was not from here. I pretended to be.

I didn't tell them:

what counts is the other tongue, and those who know how to speak it,

what counts is freedom and prison

And the freedom in prison

Us in freedom and in prison,

What counts is death and life,

Us in life and in death

What counts is murder and knowledge.

I kept myself from saying what I was thinking in secret outside the circle, up in a tree, astride a branch above the school. Instead of this, for a whole year, I ape. For twelve months I feign February twelfth. I act out the end, I lie about it, I dress it up, I clown it to the center of the universe, ah! I degrade it, I can't help myself, I fashion it into a flip-through story, I flip through it, I wanted—by climbing and degrading, by wrenching myself free from the blood, the fires, the screams—to regain my right to the world of ignorance. I do not love this world, I do not esteem it, I do not regret it, and yet I aspire to it. It is not that I desire it, it is that I fear the other. I feared so much the welcoming solitude, I thought, that I tried to accept and to make myself be accepted by the female citizens of the school. Out of fear I desired what I didn't want.

I tried to go backward. Instead, I distanced myself from both worlds, I distanced myself from ignorance, I distanced myself from knowledge. I descend, I descend, I can hardly help myself, I am on the slope of my own disappearance, as long as there is one step to descend, I will descend it, there is always another, there will have to be one that is the last, I tell myself weakly, frightened by my degradation,

there is no last step,

now I watched my companions from the bottom floor, they who hadn't changed, who were still living at their parents' house, they who hadn't lost a thing and I had another secret, I was no longer me, not at all, I was a facsimile, a phantom whose death I weakly wished for,

I who had endured the tempest of the end.

I discovered the monotonous suffering of the without end, the monotonous bitterness of sin.

I learned the unhappiness without end of the locked-up, aphonic liar: we have sold our breath to the devil, we can no longer speak, the liar is immersed in the unavowable, deprived forever of the one he was, he is drowned alive, and he never comes back up.

Only my father could have saved me, only my father would have accorded me the punishment that would break the evil spell, I dreamed of all-powerful spankings that would soundly thrash my offense. I would have died, my shame would have died. And I would have finally had the right to a resurrection.

But I had lost him. Entirely. In the present, in the future, in the past.

I lost him everywhere. And what he left me when he went away—his death, the keys, and all my chances—my meanness squandered it all in just twelve months' time.

I didn't know how to love this February twelfth. I was angry. They hadn't told me about the eagle that swallows the sun, the star that falls into a pail. They hadn't told me about the beginning hidden behind the end and about the book inside the death certificate. I mistook the end for my end. I was angry at being executed.

We are ten years old. At this age everything still takes place in our body. A father doesn't leave outside us but through us, by opening a window in our own torso. We give way to death. And since he dies through me, in the confusion of sufferings I do not distinguish his flesh from mine.

The day of the explosion, in the war I lost my arms, my legs, my father's stature, his slender back and his horse's rump, this left me gasping, I still feel the lost body today.

For years (and maybe still today), I carried my incurable, war-wounded body inside my body. The one that had waged war against me without having declared it, I've always said so, it was God who attacked me, and I've always stuck to it. I filed a complaint, I was in the right.

Yes, but I wouldn't complain of this today. Neither of the blows nor of the wounds.

It was a timely death. It fell at the wrong time, yes, but on the other hand, at the right time.

At the right time, I must affirm it this year, 1989, as never before.

At ten years old, the child can go mad and no one will tell her that it takes a misfortune thirty years, sometimes fifty, to become a chance. The greatest misfortune in the world befell me in the moment I was expecting it the least. A few months older, I would have defended myself. This was a death just in time for me to receive it right in the chest, awake, without help, without anesthesia. God tore half my ribs from me and lacerated half my lungs.

If I had known. But luckily we never, ever know what a great misfortune has in store for us. *Alles ist weniger, als es ist, alles ist mehr.*

If I had known, would I have fallen less far, and then would I have never learned what I discovered down there?

The author: But we never know. We walk in such darkness and we never know if we are the child, the father, the grandmother, the dwarf, the conqueror, at what moment, who we are, and how much, and more or less than who. We play a part in a famous play every day, and in the end that is not at all the part we play, it is not Cleopatra, it is Brutus and it is another play, and often we are played in two or three plays that are being performed at the same time. The hero of our existence is obviously our father, we think, until the day when we think the exact opposite. Our father was hiding the true hero from us, our mother.

And the person we love most in the world and for whom we paid at the entrance to the path, in a single stroke, with our whole life, and in cash, we don't know if it is really she, or why we love her, but we love her with a wonderful sureness. This is the only way to advance.

And how do we advance?

In darkness, says the author, and we call it broad daylight. But one day after twenty years we fall into a pit, or we run into a wall. We turn around. And we see the path we have been forging for twenty years. It is altogether another! And we laugh. And we start out again in an altogether other direction. We think. This time, it really is daylight, we think. It could happen. You never know.

———

I spent a day with Melchior, the author recounts. Melchior, the king of a kingdom where she will never go. A seven-year-old King. He said: "I am sight impaired." They spent the whole day, side by side, she coming from the country of books, he coming from the kingdom on the other side, like two strangers united by their strangeness, in an agitated, agile contact that transformed them from one quarter of an hour to the other into another animal species—this, this was the work of Melchior, who had taken hold of the author's body so as to swim, to climb, to nest space, and to make of their two bodies one human being. "I am a free-floating character," said Melchior. "You cannot ask me to play this role or the other."

Melchior got to know the author with his hands, he fluttered around her like two birds and drew her with a deft line. And in the same way the author got to know the weight and skin of Melchior. But she was less free. Less bird, less fish, less air.

And Melchior had second sight. He was free to see all he did not see and all he showed the author. He saw the entrance to a closed cave that the author hadn't seen. Wondering why it was placed so high up in the white wall and what was behind the door. The author wondered where the door was, the one she couldn't see but that existed in another kingdom. Melchior swam, flew, and hopped very fast. Neither light nor darkness. "I am second-sight impaired," thought the author, I am not a free-floating character, because I am without the kingdom of Melchior. And I only manage to have a little second sight in certain chapters of my books. Tell me again what you see, said the author. And with his magician's freedom, he described for her a great number of people, as he saw them. He has the right. But we are the second-sight impaired: without rights, unavowed, and presumptuous.

Once arrived at the bottom of my abasement, at the very bottom, there is nothing left. For months I take photographs of my fellow female citizens and of my teachers, with a camera in which there is no film: this was my longest and my greatest act of defiance. This crime surpasses my imagination. I am the empty camera, the empty body, the empty eye. At the very bottom there is no more age or sex or love: the impotent hatred watches the world that thinks nothing, with empty eyes. My silent chuckling like the demon who hates hell. What I feel for months: the hellish pain of nothingness. I machine-gun my teachers with an empty weapon. Ghost that I am, I take phantom photos of ghosts. And I utter ghostly howls of defiance at life's madness.

There was absolutely no one in the secret: not even me, who didn't know what I was doing. I dance for months in a flameless fire.

The author was born from my ashes. From the incombustible anger amid my ashes. I fell into the secret's tomb. And no one knows I am dead. That's the worst.

It was February twelfth, the second. I took a step. I was in the cemetery, down below. For the first time. Intimidated. I climb among the graves. Here: no one to lie to. No one's phantom photo to take. No one here has ever seen me. I am in my foreign land; shyly, I enjoy this. I climb, shaken by the idea of seeing again, of seeing, of seeing again, of meeting my foreign father: my father and the foreigner. Young, rejuvenated, I greet, I am greeted. We are among strangers here. Fountains, doves, coolness in the midst of flames, come to me. In my womb a birth is gently born.

Cemetery: my foreign country of birth. Up above, to the right occurs *the first unmeeting,* face to face with the granite flyleaf: the stone speaks.[2] It's my father. It's impossible and it's my father. The impossible is of a great simplicity. The simplicity of the impossible takes me in its arms, and I accept. I am the daughter of the tomb for which I feel a silent, impossible love, a love that goes beyond possible love. Finally, love returns, the one that had ceased to flow. —Were you afraid to love me? asks the name of my father. —Yes, Doctor. —Were you afraid to love my skeleton? —Yes, Doctor. —But I am not only this name and this skeleton, how silly you are! —Of course, I say, exultant. —Surely you have read *Das Ding*? —Have *you* read *Das Ding*? I say. What surprised me the most was that he spoke in German, my mother's tongue. —How silly you are! Well, so you've read it, so now do you understand? —Yes, of course, I lied, exultant. (I haven't read *Das Ding*. But that the thing is everything is something I understand.) —So that's everything, I say. —That's everything. Everything and nothing but everything. Where in the devil do you think I am now? he teases me. Nowhere and only in this hole? Haven't you heard the sound of the wheels of my Citroën? In dreams? No? Well, too bad for you. Pay a little attention then when I arrive.

—I'm going to dream. Are you coming? —Mmmm —Always? —Well, there's nothing but always now.

All of a sudden I remember his way of tickling my tummy with his toes. There was the beach, his body, my body mingled. —Then you're not angry anymore, my daughter?

I had entered the cemetery rotten, used up, extinguished, expulsed, annihilated by me. I emerged on the other side.

Nothing is what we think.

That day, everything started by being a little less, a little more, not altogether what it is,

I heard him in each sentence, I heard a little less a little more than the sentence, I heard his skeleton and his foreign echo,

space multiplied, everything a little farther a little closer and not altogether here nor there,

and me, too, not altogether me, not altogether she, a little more and a little less than what I am, a little younger a little less young, a little less a little more woman

and the person I love—she is not and she is,

on this February twelfth, I began to bear the tremor

I couldn't do otherwise.

Just before my father's death, I almost died of desire for a doll. She was veiled. I never saw her face. How can one want to die for someone whose beauty one can only guess at? She had everything I die for, but what, I didn't know how to say.

The author dreams: the pretty little brunette girl that I was, I see her leave and go into a store. I hurl myself in her pursuit. Go into the store. She isn't there. I exit quickly. Maybe she went inside next door, will she come out again?

I wait in vain. Never again will I see clearly, keenly, the pretty little girl that I was: she's disappeared.

February, my womb, my tomb, will I complain, will I complain of my mourning?

February, my precipitation, will I cry out they have torn from me my father's long paws, they have cut from me my father's long bird neck, they have sliced off my arm, a whole body has been detached from my body, will I take fright?

Come on, Truth, show us your teeth—how white they

are! your teeth, how merry they are!—and help us to hear the oboes and the clarinets, life's companions!

Would I like to be one of those who are infirm with father, one of those people who still have their father stuck to their ankles,

with a father who catches them by the legs, a father who sits astride their face, a heavy old jealous father who massacres them and sucks their marrow, a father with a bone in his mouth who looks at them funny at their slightest movement, an enraged father who oversees the smallness and the infirmity of his daughter?

And who have no other world, and this one, the only one, with its low ceiling, crushing their skulls?

No, my father fell at the right time, neither too early nor too late. I had a good cry. This was a happy, unadulterated loss, and it opened the way for me. I didn't know it right away: to start with, I had a good long cry for some twenty-odd years.

An angel reconstructs in haste the evil rich man's wall, which was damaged in a storm. The same angel destroys in one night a righteous poor man's house, sets the stable on fire, and burns the few livestock to a crisp.

Time and time again, in order to achieve a goal we pass through its opposite, the passage takes years, we feel greatly irritated.

Without my father to give me death, without death to give me the keys to the main gate, access to all the access ways, without my father to break my walls and my bones, what would have happened to me?

Today is your father's birthday, says my mother. My mother of whom I barely write a thing because between her and me, barely any paper.

"You know, if your father had lived, we would have gone to Israel," my mother says every year. Every year I forget this.

Last night an angel burned the father-dreamer's ship. He had spent all the war years assembling each little piece of the ark. In the morning there was nothing left. Neither ship nor dreamer.

I forget my father's dream. I forget it, I forget him. It was only a dream, I wake myself. A dream of death. I mean to say: a dead man's dream.

My mother doesn't say: "Today we celebrate the exodus from Egypt, our birthday." She says: "We would have gone to Israel." This is how we tell the truth, when we are our mother: one thing means another, but the angel sees to it that we do not know this. This is how we tell the truth, on the condition of not telling it.

No, I won't complain. I have an ancient admiration for the demon saint whom night ruins for us. I weep for the harm he does us, and confidently, I wait.

———————————

I extracted my knowingness, my foreign knowingness, from February twelfth, the author said to herself, my knowingness who knows a little less than herself, a little more.[3]

———————————

It was February twelfth, 1989. The author was reading *A Child* by Thomas B. In the fifth volume of his autobiography, after adolescence, after the mournings, after the disappearance of father, mother, grandfather, Thomas B. got around to his childhood: childhood, we get there in the end. I mean to say the true, the secret childhood that was confiscated and ruined for us during apparent childhood, the kingdom of which we were dispossessed at the very time when we were the most queen the most king—of which we are, in every era, dispossessed. And it is in that time that everything was given to and inflicted on us one hundred-fold: happiness and unhappiness, enigma and revelation, omnipotence and impotence, all together and with a crushing blow, death and births.

On the first day the Child passed alone before the cemetery. (Me alone with my brother. The cemetery is *on the way*. We have to pass by there. *O mors spes et victoria*. By the foreign tongue, the one that speaks to me in morse species and victoria code.)

On the second day same story, in another way: the Child took off on his bike to go *into* the cemetery to his friend's funeral. But we never get there. On the way we pick some flowers. A young man bounds out of the forest (I recognize the woods), throws us on the ground, and undertakes to demolish our engine with an ax. He strikes our spokes, our handlebars, our fenders, the bell, our bell, our trumpet, steals and vanishes, spits on us the absolute spittle—and leaves us for dead. For we have died of this spittle, decapitated by spittle. The Child has the impression it was a Czech or a Pole. The angel. So came the foreigner with the ax, and all this in childhood already.

"Hey," says my mother, "you know who died today, we've just been informed? The one you're reading. That Thomas B." This is what happens: we're reading a child and we're informed of his death.

"So it is *he* who died for my birthday," the author tells herself, without being able to think more precisely, without being able to feel the loss, or the sorrow. Because for forty years, this day, February twelfth, had never been lived in this world, but in the other. It was always, she sensed it, a day of another temporal nature from the other days. A window open onto eternity. She was in the middle of reading him when he "died." In her hands and under her eyes. The author continued to read. Thomas B. continued to live otherwise.

The author thought of the funeral: it is there, in the cemetery, before the open grave, that Thomas B.'s loss would be felt. Because no one in the world ever knew how to attend a funeral as strongly, as furiously, with such vitality. In each book he goes to a funeral. He bewitches the funeral, he makes it speak, he makes it avow. At the funeral, everyone avows: the dead, the living. Funerals don't only take place at the cemetery. They start at home, they finish at the inn, they start in the middle of existence and come to a close on the last page, and he, he is the exhumer, the exhumer of all we bury, but that in truth is already buried, and that we merely rebury. He'll be missed at his own funeral, the author thought. And for a moment she felt the loss and the sorrow. She imagined the dead man's solitude and his sorrow. And she felt sorry. But for the rest, he would be missed nowhere: everywhere he has thought, obviously he remains. What was confiscated from him was his own funeral. One or two hours of impotence. And of annoyance as well, because they would do better to bury the burial, in order to spare him an awkward moment. But they will not do this. They will bury him: they will want for once to attend his funeral.

So it is on February twelfth that Thomas B. will have written the last page of the book that he was and that he is. Thomas B. has just died, this didn't surprise her, there was nothing unexpected, he's only just finished (the book of his death) dying (this book), his autobiography, writing the last page —Life, death, writing merged in a single effort . . .

So it is today that Thomas B. wrote the last page: a life contained between two stones of paper.

He always wrote his books as a future corpse, with his contemporaries for matadors.

Tearing Down the Wall, a Work of Angels

Has Thomas B. entered my other country today? No, he was always there. The country inhabited by my inhabitants, the one my father promised me. People I would've never dreamed of approaching while they were alive enter, sometimes, in the very moment I turn toward them as toward people essential to my existence, forever indissociable from my taste, my mobility, my view, enter, suddenly, my other country. This is what happened between Clarice Lispector and me: the moment I turned in her direction, she passed over to the other side. December tenth. She left me December tenth's fifty-seven oboes—and the echo of her galloping stars to listen to at four o'clock in the morning before the world. For twelve years, at four o'clock on the mornings of December tenth, I've been listening.

Is unavowable: the mute idea for which I reproach myself severely: that something in me is in a strange rapport of sorcery with certain people who, they, obscurely know what they are still far from knowing: the date of their own death. These people, often women, let unreadable lines pass between their sentences. Conceive a secret, one that would be torn from nature and inscribed in an unknown tongue. And something in me receives, unbeknownst to me, the message in this other tongue. But all this comes to pass within our natural darkness. Atoms telephone atoms.

Why, I ask, did Thomas B. die on my birthday?

And you're surprised that I'm surprised? Coincidences affect us, like certain first names that have pursued us for decades or certain syllables that will not fail to make a secret cord resonate as soon as we reach an as-yet-unknown port, a novel that promises to become flesh of our flesh, or the woman or the author we will nevermore cease to adore.

And how to measure the mystery of having a name as strange as the author's, who is called Hellia. Hellia with an *h*. A name with the only silent letter in the French language. But in her mother's tongue it is just the opposite: the letter of aspiration. Extinguished in this country, helloing in the other. And it is by its ladder that she passes, with a breath, from one tongue to the other, from silence to the burst of laughter. What this name has made her do, we will never be able to say. What it swears in one tongue, it forswears in the other. Too much hell, too much light, too much chance suspended above her head. This is why the author renounces measuring. Her name above her head, now promise now threat, and the promise is itself the threat. Because of this axe-like *H,* glimmering to her North.[1] And opening for her the way.

Between the author and these characters who became, at the first stroke of book, her intimates, there is death: the whole expanse of death. This is what allows the author and her character to unite.

I had barely begun to read *The Passion according to G.H.* when I received the news. Sadly, I watched this woman leave, sadly, enviously. Growing distant, she grew large. It was I who was surrounded by shadows. Is unavowable: this obscure, sad jealousy toward these great travelers, the chosen.

Is unavowable: the desire, concealed behind the most distant thought, to know their fate.

Is unavowable and scandalous: the thought: to be dying today. To have this chance: the freedom of the dying—to enjoy this, me, too. For if I were dying . . .

(I leave to the author the entire responsibility for this scandal, for I, I am a woman who has always obeyed all interdictions.) For if I were dying (says the author), if the last day were promised me, and if then I were young and vigorous,

if I were halfway standing up in the boat of the great travelers, in broad daylight, and if then I could write, how I would sing of life's mysteries, how I would say all I do not say, how at last I would celebrate love and its madness, how I would find the violence, the laughter, the huge breath so that I might be born at last in a foreign land and meet myself over there—whereas today my own birthday is still that of others as well, in this very moment I kill myself by not killing the others (says the author)—

is unavowable: the thought: it is then—only one day away from the door—that we breathe, I who endlessly hold my life's breath, I who hold in my cries of terror and my cries of pleasure for fear of frightening the neighbors and my loved ones,

is unavowable: the thought: I ask to die for a time so as to have the chance to live, if not to tell the story of my life,

For when I die, thinks the author, won't I have the right to be myself? On the last day, won't we disentangle ourselves, you and I? And then we will see clearly who I am.

The author has a passion for doors. All doors: doors to mystery. From the first closed door, the almond-green door of Mémé, the grandmother, always closed, door to the mystery of grandmothers, at which we must knock, knock.

All those women who give way to the other side: books. Is absolutely unavowable: the passion for books, the ferocity, the need, the exultation, the haste to flee the places inhabited by those people close to me, in order to regain the poets and other characters, in their books.

And there is even the haste to regain the poets living far from themselves, at the heart without human limits of their own collection.

What is reading? It is unavowable. What confusion! In the middle of the house we open the white door and we're no longer here. Where are we in broad daylight, elbows resting on the familiar table? In Egypt, and in the same stride, in Austria—and in the same stride in Osnabrück where no one knows if I have ever been. In the other world and from one country to the other everyone speaks the same language. In the foreign world, without which I could not live, thinks the author, and to which I venture, unavowably to the call of foreigners whom I love with a foreign love. Love foreign to my loved ones, and to myself.

Is unavowable: the escape in broad daylight.

And in the same stride to Rembrandt's in the Amsterdam atelier. Where for thirty years the author has been obliged to venture when necessary and without explanation.

Is unavowable: the secret of these meetings that have never ceased to occur, despite apparent interruptions. Rembrandt has always returned, and she to him. It is a matter of a certain kinship at a distance. Foreign kinship, infinitely faraway. It is a matter of a resemblance at an infinite distance, dating, I am sure of it, from the origin.

But what then do they have in common, this man born on *July 15, 1606,* in Leyden to a family of nine children, Catholic then Protestant, to a family with a homeland passed on from generation to generation, and that knows no uprooting, his grandfather sowed wheat, his father is a baker

and this woman born on *June 5, 1937,* in Oran to a family that is Jewish from the South Jewish from the North, to a family with seven lost homelands for a cradle, with dis-inheritance for an inheritance, and for a landscape, a no-man's-land.

Nothing apparently.

I search now with a sure eye over these maps of destiny for: faces. Nothing obviously in common. I lean over. I take up an eyeglass. And there, in the eyes, I see—something . . . sparkling—an absence. There is: a point of departure. The trace of a gaze that travels afar, beyond centuries, toward the distant door, that travels toward the Orient. I see: a direction. Where does it lead us? We will not know, if we let ourselves be discouraged by the length of the gaze. We must journey a long time in pursuit of this gaze. Departing from Amsterdam already headed for 1624. For the other origin.

It is a matter of the origin from before, the second ori-gin or the first, the veiled but ineffaceable one, toward which certain people draw their lives like a bow.

It is this foreign origin that is the painter's secret. She—the origin—has always been there. The unknown Source of his force. The foreigner who plants the lacerating desire for the next painting like a knife into his breast. Who are you? Where are you? I feel you breathing hard behind my back, but I turn around in vain. From painting to painting, it is toward her—this origin—that he goes, the one he cannot do without, that he trembles with fear each time of losing, of not regaining before the door, and who is here, the one who doesn't obey him, she comes, and he can do nothing about it, the one who is stronger than he and who calls on him to travel farther than himself.

Who is it? the foreign mother, the bride?

And how to explain to his wife why Orientals come into his paintings, and why his Dutch characters are bedecked with turbans and crests?

And his whole life he paints in a foreign land inside his family, *hinaus in die Fremde der Heimat,* leaving through the painting's door, in the foreign breast hidden inside the homeland, orientally, passing through the painting's door and with a single brush step he is already deep inside the Holy Land, deep inside, in the very thick of Jerusalem.

Hendricje is before the open door, and although he paints her at the door, with his brush in the thick of she who is also the door, he departs for afar, for so far away . . . toward the inner Orient, that he doesn't know, but this Orient knows him and awaits him, like the last mother, the bride.

Between the painter and her, it is a matter of distancing in broad presence, and conversely of a poignant love for presence, because it is so threatened.

There has always been a Rembrandt. And if the author feels funny saying so, it's because on top of everything she doesn't like painting. What she loves in the work of Rembrandt is that it isn't about painting, it's about embarkation, it's about freedom and prison, about the freedom inside the prison that is painting. And about the painter's escape.

One day long ago when the author wanted to die, day of error, whose date I have forgotten, day when the author wasn't herself, day when the author, in a fit of total error, no longer recognized anyone and above all not herself, day when the author no longer saw any difference between the person she loved and a demon of a dazzling cruelty, and rather than seeing no difference, rather than seeing herself love a demon, the author in a fit of total terror preferred to go mad, preferred to lop off the world one meter away from her, at the moment when there was no longer anyone around her and when memory and love didn't stretch beyond a one-meter-long radius around her, at the moment when only an angel's embrace can tear us from the transparent arms of death,

on that day, by chance, there was, on the table, open

by chance, Rembrandt in the person of *The Jewish Bride*. There was something in *The Jewish Bride*, something in Rembrandt, that diverted the course of her madness. Something Jewish, something bride-like, something of a woman protected from falling by the balustrade of an arm.

It was the portrait of the Bride who is not afraid. The author saw that Rembrandt had painted the truth. She saw the hand that *is*. Nothing was symbolical, or allegorical, or biblical. It was about real people. One could believe. What was beautiful was that the bride and bridegroom of *The Bride* were not very beautiful: they were not impossible. The author was bathed in the incredibly soft light of possibility.

And yet the one I love the most, thinks the author, is the slaughtered one. The one that loses its head. The one that wouldn't have saved me. The one that shows me passion's path, the one that opens its chest, the one that is mad for truth. But it is not out of love that I love it. It is out of necessity.

It isn't only with Rembrandt that I feel myself to be in this unavowable, foreign kinship. But equally with close or unknown people in whom I perceive the traveling gaze.

In pursuit of this gaze that departs from the Ukraine, I take my leave, I follow the gaze to the end of the Universe, to the disaggregation of atoms.

In pursuit of this gaze that departs from the shores of the Mediterranean. The journey will be unavowable. Unavowably long.

This is why a woman who has children, like myself, would never make such avowals. She would keep silent until death.

But the author has no children. Let's go, Truth, my ferocious bride, show us your oh-so-merry teeth. No children, say I, and no mother. I take up my pen and my boat, I open the door, I am gone, from seven o'clock in the morning till nightfall, I follow an ecstasy of absence. No one knows my destination, chains, alliances, correspondences, I deny, I break, I burn, I am lost, I am saved, without address, without name, without pity,

if on my dress there are traces of birdlime, of sperm, of blond adopted children's diarrhea, I rip my dress off, if on my dress is one of those children I carry without noticing, one of those tiny green parasites clamped to my white skirt with its tiny ivy fingers, I seek to detach it so as to place it on the ground. But the tiny thing doesn't want to let go. Its puny voice cries out: "I'm afraid." "Well, but let me put you on the floor." I manage neither to reassure the poor tiny thing nor to detach it properly: trying to unfasten it, I break its tiny bits of crumbly leaf. There will be enough left just the same, I say, and I rip off my parasited dress. Ah! the babies: at ninety years old I will still find some stuck to my wall.

My body, disengaged from the leaves and scrap iron, is of a perfect speed: I don't feel it, with this body I am virgin, I leave and I don't return, I am happy beyond happiness.

I write. In the house I am a character from my mother's dreams, my mother who is alive and who brings me a plate of raw vegetables at noon. Meanwhile, with the unknown violence of the slaughtered ox, *I* lead my lives in a foreign land.[2] And I don't even know it.

We adopt the direction. And very quickly we go so far as to forget the main characters of our known existence. By the end of an hour, sometimes less, we no longer see when we turn around those whom we seem to hold on to as to our own organs, as to our eyes, as to our hands. One journey and we forget our son, our daughter, our mother.

And at this very instant, the author has just willingly forgotten her brother. She had just taken off when he arrived.

She acted as if she didn't see him, and she hadn't seen him, she continued to think only of her book, next to which her brother was, then, absolutely nothing or no one

(but I didn't do it on purpose, I believed, sincerely, I'm sure of it, he was going to stay until the evening and until tomorrow, and survive my slight but profound assassination attempt, and I was sure, I didn't even think about it, that this minimally violent scene would vanish later on, as if it had never taken place, I hoped, without even taking the trouble to hope, to pass through the web—the web of what—of the last Judgment),

such a small assassination, she barely thought, she didn't even think, and we commit so many. But look: this didn't come to pass at all as hoped, to the contrary, her brother was surely hurt, perhaps, yes,

and all of a sudden at three o'clock, he brusquely ripped open the door behind which we had hidden, the book and I, and he said with a stroke of his big sonorous voice: I am leaving.

This is what the author wanted, this is what the sister didn't want.

Oh, the crime fell on me, the sister. The old crime the first. My brother didn't spare me, he struck me with three words: "I am leaving. Yet again you have killed me yet again."

And how could I have known that one doesn't let go of one's brother's hand in the cool, deserted town, without a jeep passing by at the very same moment and mowing my brother down, look at me, cries the jeep, I am death with her scythe, and with a blow it mows down my brother, my innocence, and the totality of my freedom in advance. Could I have known this when I was five years old in the deserted Oran street and he four years old in 1942, and I didn't know what the debarkation of the Americans would mean for me, the joy, the freedom, the white bread, and conversely the terror and the cogged wheels of punishment?

And how could I have known that this scene would forever crouch between us, my brother and me, and that I could never again not extend my hand to him without the immediate arrival of a jeep and a scythe, never again?

I watched him go—him and the one he used to be—him today with his big voice, him with the one he used to be, the child of 1942 emerging from the teeth of the jeep skinned alive, his cry gripping my cry, and I couldn't even tell them I was sorry, his cry planted in my throat.

I watched him go, carried off by the foreign crowd, above me, far from me, as if he weren't anyone, a slaughtered beast, as if he weren't mine and I didn't exist. All I saw was the howling. Between the two of us the cry, the cry of brother to sister and of sister to brother.

And I couldn't tell him I was sorry. When there is assassination, this is the sign: "Amen" remains stuck in our throats. Whose assassination? cried the author. And the words remained stuck in our throats.

The two of us were silent. The two of us denied. It had always been about the two of us, since forever.

We lied, "You're going? I didn't know you were going, it doesn't matter, I'm leaving," we told the truth, it didn't matter,

but today's truth had no strength: in vain I affirmed it, I didn't believe it.

What time is it, what age, what year, what scene is casting its confusion over each one of my spoken words, and my voice pales? Let's act out again the scene we mustn't think of, the one I'm thinking of, I don't want to think, and I don't know if he's playing at it, I never know if he's still playing a trick on me: the scene starts up again, I take a step, the jeep arrives.

The car carried him off, a big Renault full of dogs, as if he would never return, in vain he told her: I'll be back—

when?—some evening—you'll be back? said the frightened sister, as if whether he would return still depended on her, death was between us,

once again we were united by this crime that made us more brother more sister than ever, a crime which together we were trying and without saying anything not to think of.

And all this because of you, my bridegroom, my hidden love, my hoped-for book for which I sacrifice mother and brother. And sister, too. And more still.

But I am innocent, I do know that, says the author, I wasn't driving the jeep, and naturally we—all us sisters—have the right to let go of our brother's hand in the street in 1942. There was no one there, neither car nor motorcycle. And the right to close the office door when our brother arrives unexpectedly forty-seven years later and in the moment when we have just, after long months of torment, arrived at last near to our secret love.

No harm done.

After all, I cannot say I'm sorry for an assassination attempt that didn't even take place.

We were inseparable. A jeep, come from I know not where . . .

But I do know that it's not at all like that. The crime is not what we think. It's enough to let go of the hand and the harm is done. Your brother's hand.

Because if it had been my cousin, the wound would have healed. But it was my flesh, that is to say my childhood, that is to say, for it must be said, it was I to my misfortune and to my good fortune, coauthor of our times in the garden when we were crouched, seen from the sky, two mushrooms, two pups, the sister's dark gaze fixed on the wide-open eyes of the brother, like the bridegroom's hand

on the hand of the Jewish bride, and when it was a matter—
for the two of us—of fashioning the entire world out of
earth, pebbles, and branches: for the two of us, god on earth
as only one.

It is the story of all the mistakes, the creations, the
escapes we have accomplished, in having been sister and
brother, like unto each other. And about the solitary mistake.

If it had been my cousin, but I was sister, born sister,
and therefore brother, and thus it was me whom I slaughtered alive, it is the brother inside the sister, the brother outside the sister, I the jeep, I victory, I the Allies, and to the
contrary, the Allies against the born allies that we were, sister and brother, the two of us against the entire world.

And ever since then I am here, brooding over the
slaughtered one, inside me and outside me, my whole existence spent slaughtering him, slaughtering myself, and
brooding over him, good and evil entangled like the brother
gripping the sister by the cry.

And the brother?

His repeated attempts to assassinate, later on and for
years, the sister's person,

Don't count,

The race in the garden, with the iron bar in the brother's hand, doesn't count,

since it was the jeep that started it.

My concern is with the crime. My brother's concern is
with revenge.

In life, as soon as I say the words *my brother*, the stage
is set. Some murders assassinate us.

While I am attempting to avow the crime I didn't commit but that one day entered my life and never left, I realize
I am perhaps in the process of writing, without wanting to,
the Book of Innocence.

Innocence, our mystery. Our dream.

Our mother sends her two children to get milk.

Upon leaving we come across the scene of the bird that is taking place in the shadows. The mother bird is cleaning her bird. The little one has a little wound on its little belly to the right. The mother cleans the little wound with cotton, her beak tilted, her eyes grave.

The exclusion of any indication of time and place suggests that in *The Death of the Bird* the mythic story is at the action's origin. We are seized by a sort of dread. The little one on its back, the mother rubbing and cleaning the wound, we tell ourselves she must be harming it, but clearly the baby bird isn't crying. In order to do a better job the mother adroitly tears out with her beak all the little feathers around the wound. In sum, she plucks it, we think. The memory of *The Anatomy Lesson* renders the sight of this body plucked by the energetic beak particularly horrible. But apparently it has to be this way. Gently, the little one offers no resistance. When the mother has finished, she turns it over. It is then we see that it hasn't a feather left on its entire body. It is much more serious than I had thought. I didn't know what it was to be cared for in this way, shivers the author, at the sight of this little, red, naked, consenting thing.

Meanwhile, the baby bird turns its beaming face toward us. "Is it OK? Am I beautiful?" Oh yes, you are beautiful! Love beams from this morsel of flesh. And all this, this stripping has been done with so much love. This couple can be detached from the mythic action and become a symbol. "Am I beautiful, am I loved?" asks the dying beast. Oh yes, we say, you are filled with love, we say leaning with love and pity over the beast who dies with a big smile.

But after all, we are not birds, we mustn't judge. We do not know what it is to expire beneath the beak of love.

We are always in the midst of killing and of being killed almost every day. Everything is our mistake. Our innocence made up of all the mistakes we haven't made.

In this painting from his last years, Rembrandt's passion acquired an independent value. And we never know from whence comes the light, from whence the darkness.

Is my book going to be a death I will have given myself in order to write better? thought the author, transfigured with horror. And the most dreadful is the mix of horror and radiance that make this canvas strangely endearing.

The author:
There is death between those I love and me, death, my death coveted, refused, the veiled woman I wanted to die for just before my father's death. And yet I didn't die for her, because my father didn't pay the slightest attention to my mortality. Because I'm the dead one, he sensed.

I who am condemned to live, I envy those who are going to die. Those who receive a letter very early on.

I've been wanting to say that for a long time.

You who have received the letter, you who are mortal, you who believe you are, imagine—no, you can't imagine it—the fate of those who are doomed to immortality. Half the tortuous pleasures of life are refused us. We are abandoned each year, we are dropped onto the earth, and for a mistake we haven't even made we are left before the door.

When I received the news of Thomas B.'s death, I uttered a cry of admiration. He succeeded! A man who prophesies his end might be mistaken, might—without meaning to—be lying to himself. But he knocks on the door, with all his might, and the door opens. I uttered a cry of admiration. "Where are you going?" I cried. "Is that any of your concern?" he hurls back at me. I heard for the first time his beautiful, deep cantor's voice. And he leaves. A man I had never loved, but in that instant I loved him out of admiration. "Is that any of your concern?" And he leaves. If he were alive, I would hate him. But hatred doesn't enter the house of the dead. The door in my face, I listen to him going. And nothing is left me but to love him.

———————

—All those who have knocked on the door with all their might and in the end the door swings open.

—If you want to die, knock.

—But I'm afraid to knock loud enough. I don't want to de-I me. What I would have liked is to receive the letter that others have received. And then, right here, in this world, to be, while I'm alive, someone from the other world. The wall has just been torn down. Flat on our bellies, atop the rubble, we enjoy the absolute freedom of the dead who are still alive.

Then, for more or less several months, we see everything, we see at last from one side the two faces of each thing, we see the evil visage of good and the demon's charming smile, we see the error of truth and we see the innocence in each crime, at least that's what I imagine, it is then that we understand that we have never understood a thing, that no matter how far we go in pursuit of truth, when we have accomplished the last step we are allowed to take with our last strengths, she—truth—is one step ahead, she is always one step away from us, and all we will be able to do is to head in her direction, and we understand that we have never accomplished love's last step because the last step is no longer love's, and we see the two eyes of the faces of things, one is brown the other is gray-green, but on closer look it's the opposite, but this is nothing, one looks toward the without, the other toward the within, and we see we have spent our lives giving to those who gave us next to nothing and receiving from people to whom we give next to nothing, we nourished one person, and we were nourished by another person, there was nourishment, and there was hunger, and "next to nothing" is not what we think, and receiving is the mirror in which the person who gives sees herself giving, and certain people love to see themselves rewarded with reflections, but others cannot stand it, and certain people prefer to receive in the same measure that they give, and that's impossible, almost every person who gives would like to receive, and at the same time likes not receiving, and we have always given infinitely less than what we would have liked to give, because giving gives the desire to give; and even so more than we think we have given, and what comes to pass inside the other, in her house and in her heart, we never absolutely know, a discovery that would drive us mad with anguish (I continue to imagine) if we didn't understand that even so we loved to give thus and to receive, like blind people, we were unable to do otherwise, and that in the end we loved more, and loved less, than we had thought, and in the end we loved those we had thought we didn't want to love, and this error, this injustice, is the very way of love, and we were always paid back and punished not according to our merits and our mistakes but according to grace, we were lauded for what cost us nothing, and for what almost cost us our skin, nothing at all, we answer for the crimes we are accused of but not for those we are not accused of, and we need images, we cannot live without our images, we need to be depicted or described or represented, and sometimes what we will be able to do best for a person is her portrait, minute, tireless, because it is not enough for us to have been born to be in possession of our existence, we want to be looked at, we want to enjoy our éclat, mother, tell me I am beautiful, give me the word that gives, sing me the legend of Me, make the éclat of my ugliness beam, the mystery of my blackness, offer me the anguish that pierced me, the wounds, the terrors, the assassinations, draw them on canvas with brilliant words, I want everything, even shame, provided that it be: me. I don't want to cross the world without my face and without my keys, a painter! a painter! may I be accorded my own substance, O palms, diamond, my sparkling brother tell me about my eyebrows, my astonished lips, paint the portrait of my youth.

———————

Yes, what we could give of most loving to a person, that is to say of most giving, I imagine this would be her portrait *in truth*. We must let ourselves be guided by severity. It is this (this severity we need to use against our cowardices) that I am in despair of ever reaching during my lifetime.

I who my whole life have been afraid of killing with spoken words, and then afraid of being plucked and eaten, and next afraid of hurting, if I received the letter I will never receive, I would give myself over to severity. I would paint pain, lies, calculation, escape, protection, regret, the infirmity hidden in strength, and the strength that sprouts from infirmity, and above all I would paint forgiveness.

Because, I am sure of it, what the torn-down wall reveals will make us smile and forgive. Don't you see how we have fought for so many years to emerge from the night, and we've never succeeded at it, because during those same years we fought to remake the night and we did succeed at that, and this in spite of ourselves and against ourselves.

The author stops here. Because from the other side one sees what she cannot imagine. Here her jealousy starts. What Clarice Lispector saw on December 9, 1977, was a landscape seen from her chest where flowers were sprouting: white lilies. Landscape seen with her dry, burning body, made for looking, but which, from here, from my life, and from my still flowerless body, I don't have what it takes to see. There is no witness.

But I'm already living me from 2989 on, ahead of me are as many and no more marvels than there are preceding me. Where will we be—my atoms, my palpitations—in 2989, where my vaporous thoughts? *I* won't know, but you, my atoms, my nacreous sweats, you will. And this non-knowledge, together with this knowledge, lends me an astonished intoxication. To be what we will be, to bear the incalculable future in our hearts as on a donkey's fidelity: this has the taste of the divine.

Am I lying? Is everything I've just written merely an authorial embroidery? I don't know. The author writes what traverses her. And in a domain as uncertain as the one where these pages are taking place, at the very edge, atop the rubble that was the wall, it isn't she, it is desire, it is hopefulness, it is childhood that writes. But desire is the beginning of Truth. The first half. Christopher Columbus's caravel was already half of America. Believing is the flesh of truth.

Can I be sure that on the day of my death I *will believe in my* 2989? On that day will I avow such a curiosity? I do not know. Won't the science of that day have confiscated my fairyland of atoms from me? And won't I be told so many times that the atom isn't alive that I'll believe it? Oh, then would I weep, oh, would I weep for the error of my entire life, for my atoms' immortality. I would weep for my forever-unknown infinity. And one last time I will renounce the veiled doll I wish to die for.

Why does the author reach the wall only to meet the limits of her breath and her power, and before her gaze the invisible begins? She has never succeeded in surpassing this wall, this ruin of limits, her treasure and her limit. Lacking strength, she doesn't manage to imitate Rembrandt in spoken words. She doesn't manage to remain in Rembrandt, in the atelier of secrets, without losing herself in there, or to find it without losing it.

And doubtless, if she happens to find it, doesn't know she has found it. But most often this takes place painfully: it is a dazzlement. She sees—she's seen. She sees no more. There is a secret. What she lacks in order to seize it is the ability to write the flash.

—I would so like to tear the wall down.

—But that is the work of the dying. A descent among the dead.

—I need to try.

—At your age, what for? says the mother.

The author feels like trying. At your age, what for? says the mother. Apparently, the blind child whose sight is returned at the age of eight goes mad with pain. He used to live inside his world's flesh, looked after by his own enchantments, and he saw colors with other colors and other names from ours. And when he reaches the age of eight we dethrone him, we destroy his kingdom forever, we kill the enchanted mother, and we toss him without eyelids before an outburst of earths, red ones blue ones green ones pour mountains and torrents before his feet, there is no longer either path or door, and he falls on foreign soil in misery, like an earthworm. He has lost power, dignity, agility. Groping, he crawls, eyes closed, toward a window, fleeing the howling lights, and he rushes, weeping, into the lost arms of his night.

—Don't touch the ax, and paint people as they are dressed, says the mother. Man cannot bear the truth, she says. Besides, he will say it is not the truth. And who knows truth? And truth's cause? Everyone wants to be fooled, that's it. That's the truth. —Says the mother who is one of the author's main authors.

And maybe, muses the author, listening to her mother with joy, maybe it is my mother in me who encourages me to content myself with little.

—My grandmother used to say: "Gumzoule Tauba: Who knows what that was good for?"[3]

It was for the best. She had nineteen children. Everything was good for something. Death, injury, anguish, joy, lying were all good for something. It was good for something. For what. Muses the author who is fond of death, death that *is,* with its enchantments. And who is fond of her mother, who doesn't know death.

"Death," says the mother. "I won't be the first. Each life must end in that. It's all for the best." Says the mother. A sole life filled solely with life. Whereas the author stretches out over thousands of years and augments her life with so many deaths, with so many dead. She doesn't know how to live without deaths, without all her dead, and without foreign bodies mixed up with her body.

My Deaths. This is what the author wanted to call this book at one time.

She would have called it: *My Dead*. We would have read: *My Deaths*.[4] And we would have thought that this book was about "my deaths," hers, her own losses of life.

But she would have started like this: "I do not know if they are my fathers or my children . . ."

But it is I, as a woman, worried as a woman, who instinctively rebuffed this desire.

A word other than the word *death* is what I'll have to find, I say. And then when you say: the dead, we do not know if it's a he or a she. And see how the word attracts the dead, especially the he's.[5]

If you write: my dead, male corpses take hold of the rope and hoist themselves onto the stage.

Write: "my lives," and it is women[6] who will come to die of joy upon the beach, I say, the sea ray will be of the absolute blue of which the sea is made, and the magnolias will toss their flower leaves along the painting's shore. I say, worried. Because for several days I've been seeing clearly that by going off in such a direction, women are making themselves scarce. There is no denying: I am surrounded by my women, I am an object dear to women, and it is men who return; they climb the stairs, and the battle blooms.

———————

Suddenly squirrel, I gain the highest one, and, passing behind the last leaves, I open my wings and take flight. Presence and absence are my wings. Impossible to separate myself from them. To transcribe my life, with one leap, invisible to myself: to be not altogether what I think I am, to escape way up there, to the last leaf, at the limit of the species. Will I accuse myself of having betrayed my loved ones?

I defend myself: Jews have the right to sin in order to save their lives, to pass outside the law, to do what a Jew doesn't do. Destruction scolds: you sin, you don't seem Jewish, you aren't Jewish, destruction passes, you are born Jewish a second time. That is being Jewish. And for women, too. Surviving is our vocation. When I flee, it is not merely in order to make the secret of the word *Jew* resonate in my French tongue, *juif fuis-je*—it is so as to better revive myself.

I defend my woman's defiance, my madness. I take flight, I land in the middle of a tongue. Inside a tongue we cannot die. Here the wind always blows, no word is motionless, the limit is not a limit, what I cannot live in one tongue, I live in the other, from one tongue to the other, and each one a mother tongue, I leap, and on a river bank or a Chinese junk, I make our victories' trumpets bloom.

It is a story of escape and navigation,

it is a story of all that can surpass our walls and our bones,

and of following, with our eyes in the text of the sky, the flight of this woman who clambers up the hill

at the hour when dragonflies give way to mosquitoes,

see the Martagon lily raise its orangy head above the anemones

see the fireflies dancing in the valley, the one where she delighted between the stalks of wheat

and like the one who, seeing Elie's chariot recede, when the carriage bolted into the sky, watched, all eyes, without distinguishing anything but a single flame.

In the same way, see the tongues crack open their doors of flesh and reveal their treasure, their singular music:

My head is spinning, I've just seen three worlds in one.

Where are we now? In what country? In what book?

It is the story of losing the thread and letting oneself be guided by the voice.

Where are we now? Above and below.

And each woman's envelope holds a poet, in other words, a traveler.

I took off, I remember: I was with the author in Rembrandt's atelier when this occurred.

It was a more and more sultry night. What he was painting was the earth, century upon century, the earthy earth, thick, filled with us, filled with our dusts, I watched him painting time, the dark, earthy red of time, and all of a sudden a nostalgia uttered its rending cry. "And now enough of this light!" I cried out, "I want the other one! Music!"

My book for a horse! But no horse for me. The horse is for Clarice Lispector.

I can only count on my own wings. I unsheathed them. Crumpled, two leaves of paper. Will I suffice? But the music merely made of me a butterfly.

Night My Foreign Life

I rested. I went to contemplate my hibiscus. I feel tied to hibiscus by an illegible message. Hibiscus are animated by sequence. One flower stretches toward victory. First one sees the soul swell the petals, folded so as to exhale. Next: exclamation of red. Now the flower is going to redescend. There is no pause between the ascension toward birth and the decline. The newly born flower followed by the flower of the next generation. Already the little breast swells. This is the announcement. She's going to shout she's going to fall. I set out again.

For two weeks the author had been intending to write a chapter called "The Ideal Story." I saw it coming. One day it was here. Like the final couplet of a poem: *beginning at the end*. Next, one has to hear the climbing, descending words. The author listens, tense, irritated. Their respiration is just behind her shoulders: it's to the right, it's to the left, a little clearer, a little faster, this way.

In the meantime, I went on ahead. I have an inspiration? I follow her. She moves faster than we do. "Come on!" That's an order. Coming from my most imperious life, from my Queen who is so authoritative, so shamefully adored that sometimes I wonder if it isn't She who would be my God. I am in her hands and more: I have her under my skin. We are with each other like delirious lovers. It is Her portrait I shall paint. Without me she is nothing. But I am flat on my belly before her like a garden of impotences. There is not one that doesn't grow its flowers in my earth.

For her I would abandon the child at my breast, infant or aging—what does it matter?—at eleven o'clock at night the need is so strong, worse than God's: God drags his prophets by the ears, by the hair, by the sleeves, but not by their contracted bowels. At eleven o'clock at night I feel her light hands grab fistfuls of my own blood, and in my body blazes a panic at the idea that she might let go of me, the oh-so-powerful mistress, the gripping ungrippable, she of the transparent fists. I'm coming, I hurry, the force of time is terrible, the sea wouldn't know how to resist the moon, I withdraw, excuse me, I murmur in turn, I'm going to bed, I lie in turn, I make my own family swallow the sands of lies and now on horseback, the hillside is glossy, I already see in the distance's distance her ample quivering advance, ah I press forward, I head for the Queen, and then:

the telephone.

No, no, ah! telephone, innocent messenger from the world I want to leave behind, incarnation, ah! telephone, no temptation, you ring in vain, over there the queen's cannon already thunders for me. —But what if it's the person you love most in the world! —I'm no longer there, I'm no longer of the world where I love the person I love most in the world, so much so that for her, for one hour spent near her I would cross three France's, for one half hour—but what if it's the person whose voice you await, trembling, you circle me like a butterfly circles a flame; all day long you don't leave me, you bring me with you from room to room and even into the bathroom, I who am but a piece of promise, you cannot live without me as if my dial were your own heart seized with astonishment and when sometimes, despite your prayers and furtive kneeling, that person doesn't call you for a day, doesn't call you for two days, on the third day the planet crumbles in a flash of mourning, the great abyss opens and instantly the years' superb scaffolding vanishes before your icy body, the construction of the world is complete, the author made a mistake . . .

at that moment I ring, I am the angel of resurrection, the acidic trumpet beloved among all trumpets, the crumbling crumbles, I am a witness, the only witness, and now, it might be her, it might be me, and you do not answer?

—O telephone, I cannot, you must understand, I am Hers, it is that time, I am given over, damned, by midnight I have to renounce everything there, body, palace, oath, in favor of my Fatal Hope.

—What's that, Fatal Hope? Is that a boat? The Flying Dutchman?

—Don't ring anymore, let me sleep, let me lie upon the desired breast. You must forgive me.

—You of all people are saying that? And love? Don't you love her?

—You can't understand. This is where I go to love her otherwise, to lose her otherwise, through other feelings.

—Is it serious? Listen, listen.

—Serious? No. It takes place beyond seriousness, beyond the city, beyond the city's parlor, beyond the Boulevard, beyond the bridge, beyond the cathedral's parlor, beyond the ancient wall, beyond the wall's parlor, over there. See, I look beyond the wall's seriousness, where roads and streets are unknown. Here the Bible begins. You recognize its landscape. One always recognizes its landscape. The landscape that we recognize without ever having seen it is this one, the one from the Bible. Oh how its roughness speaks to us. I have a goat's greediness for it. It promises us thirst, solitude, enraged hope. It delivers us wholly naked up to the existence of God.

Look: see the vast curtains of dust, see the fortresses of rock, see the round, worn backs of the Bible's hills, and before each one, without a doubt, I'll find the Arabs' tent or the Jews' tent, how to know, I never know, when I see their column leaving this land, whom I see, are these my jews or my arabs. In Her blows a confused love for those who smile at me. The sky is filled with clouds, this is what the sky is made of, of loud, of filled: aging, shedding, indelible.

I've just described to you the land I go to, a boundless dryness—I want to quench my thirst with it—is the meeting's decor. My hungers, my thirsts, I am tossed about, taken away, I cannot resist them, they will kill me, I cannot deprive them of Her. It is my beasts who command.

Let me pass! Let me pass! or I'll tear your trumpet out.

And without explanation and without stopping, and without form, and without path, I unfurl now, toward Her, in Her, in the dark heart of desire. Delighting already from all that will be. I surrender to Her, in the darkness, as though to the maddest part of myself, as Penthesilea heads for Achilles,[1] inside Achilles already down dale and dark crests, she is his and he hers in a single darkness, each one darkness for the other's desire, straight for Her, in the sumptuousness of ignorance (the word *sumptuousness* is the only one that shines in this midnight), so as to deliver myself up, so as to give myself up to her creative caprice, so as to be scattered, carved up, wed, as though at my own funereal wedding, in great pomp and without knowing what awaits me

But I know I want to play with Her, stake my known life on the one we all call "She," like we call God God, with passion, and familiarity, and without knowing She who, assured as we are only of her name, of her royalty, of her foreign femininity, of her impalpable, limited presence, of her comings and goings that measure our heart.

It can only be a She, I don't know why, why She, why me, why God.

For tonight I'm given a storm of thirty days with white flags in the sky. And accompanied by pale, flashing beasts, astonishing sketches of horses' withers, I go forth into my sought-out land, into my lost land

Accompanied by a storm of thirty ringing days, by drums, live cannons, and airplane explosions

And the white flags sweeping the sky one after the other, I set forth with greed, with glory, spitting fire white on black, to the land of the dead, the émigrés, my unknown accomplices, the representatives of all my personal nationalities

An ocean crushes its groundswells onto the sky's rocks.
Trumpets of thunder, prodigality of prophetic musics
We are animals carried on the backs of drums,
Flings effaced flags onto the field
The dragon vomits its soul, the bulls bray like donkeys
I am happy, thinks the woman, I want
This wanting wants with a strength that surpasses me
Joy spurts up in my throat
I am sad to be happy, I accuse myself, I forgive myself
To belong to two worlds, I roar. A felicity moves me
Woman of two fidelities, I avow them I celebrate them
If I must accuse myself, it's of committing dreams.

I accuse myself of being happy. Crime that much more unavowable, dreaming, for not being called a crime.

But how not to be happy? Tonight I enter the land of lost lands, the galloping lightning trumpets announce to me, immense Morse code of celestial strengths, that She reigns.

The storm grows bold, reaches every floor, spreads out over the Sky's Asia, piles victory upon victory, in the white fever forges its urgent roaring

And finally wrenches from its throat the terrible screams that only the mute utter

It is God who is mad about Her

Tonight I have a storm of giants with shofroth

My God, grant that You go quite mad!

The storm with its proud Jewish ram's voice, roars on my white heels

I crush some stars under my heels and milk spills out in long icy banners to the applause of black ivory trombones

—Where are we running to, Hellia, who are we crushing, in what land are we the exultant masters? roar the Kings' horses, horses from the books of my Bible

—To Her, who makes the rains of the dead return, and ten times one hundred generations be reborn

To the Queen who recounts the books of the prophets to the prophets

And who lets us in on the secret of where this God is hiding

The God who keeps in his pocket our secrets' twisted keys

Give me back the world, give me back a view of the world, I beseech, with my angel trio's voice, let me stare the true face of love full in the face

I've had enough of my lightless days, says the cello, take my life, give me purity

—Who are we? What are we doing? —My eyes take big gulps of Night's black wine. My big eyes ready to leap upon the coming dream.

I accuse myself of taking whatever departure comes along, as long as it carries me, the trip is my necessity; I am in a rush, in a rush. Such an obedience orders me. I would die from not obeying. Come! I obey, I am élan. Climb! I obey! Obedience is my freedom. My adversaries are dead. I want what I want. What I do I want to do, and in spite of me.

I sing the night, submission to my Queen. To be held back finally by nothing of my own: all obstacles are foreign to me.

The storm sets me down. Grandiose, sinister, dusty, the landscape is that of the building sites of Kings, where one doesn't know if one is seeing destruction or construction. And we drive along, not crossing anyone's path, over a wide surface of earth. Is it the end, the beginning? The Kings' high buildings have reddish bodies, they are still dead. Will life come? Night rests above the still inanimate sky. Well then, I must have climbed the steep stairway that cuts across Nothingness. The nameless woman who has gone on ahead is, unfortunately, incapable of progress. So slow, so clumsy. She's going to make me miss the exaltation. It was a mistake to have let her pass me, I tell myself. Finally, I decide to overtake her. When an ancient, slow, familiar woman occupies the whole width of the ladder, what to do? I simply pass on the ladder in the manner of a monkey, but remaining myself, with energy, dexterity, courtesy. And once I've passed beyond the slowness, I pursue fearlessly.

I give myself up to the frightening Queen, as if fright were my delight.

From afar She predicts to me: I will turn you upside down in the Stairway, I will throw you down between my knees, I will push you onto the dull-colored earth, I will bring you to the edge of the earth before the limitless sea. As far as the eye can see stretches lifeless, limitless water, you will seek the sea everywhere that she is not. I will envelop the countrysides in a veil of sand, so that the things of the present will seem past, over cities and towns I will stretch your nearsightedness, nothing will be seen with clarity, nothing will be heard with clarity. Each instant of your journey will be a struggle to see better what you will never see. I promise you blindness and the struggle against blindness.

She promises me everything, my saint, and everything that She promises me is what I want.

—You will have the petty annoyances of which great catastrophes are made. If tomorrow you enter the house, you won't find the kitchen. If you do find the kitchen, you will do everything backward. You will never manage to work the washing machine. Everything will be against you. The water will overflow you should have put the laundry in first. Whatever isn't undercooked will be overcooked. I will show you the discord that leads our existence. You will know everything about the time difference that organizes your story. I will make of your days a race against the clock. This may not seem like much, but this is how we die so far as to miss the very hour of our death: by not being on time at the right time. One day I read a hymn to punctuality and I adored: we miss Paradise by one minute.[2] I will explain Hell to you, Paradise's rich and clever Shadow

And what is most extraordinary in the world of time is that next we spend years, up to thirty, forty, fifty, attempting to recapture this lost minute: I shall describe for you our pain. For you see, Paradise never altogether vanished. We merely retired to within close range. Our life is but a regret that hopes, and all the while we are hoping and running, we suspect we will not get there, but we vigorously belie this suspicion, for we live from the life of this illusion. All we ask is that it hold to the end of our old age.

I am talking to you about the illusions that help maintain your daily life. But in my land I will unveil you. I will split the canvas. I will hold a mirror up before you. You will see your blindness with your own eyes. And you will see also that your right ear has come unglued from your face, and it doesn't adhere to you any more than the handle of a broken amphora. Is this what you were expecting? —No. This is new. But it isn't ugly. —Who broke your ear? —How should I know? —Well, then, speaking of range. Who knows? Without your being able to do a thing, I will make you children, countless children of all sizes and all colors, you will get blonds, blacks, vegetables, drunkards. They will fill your heart with the sugar of melancholy. One at a time, but very often. Monsters capable of anything, who run and break before even knowing how to walk, who at the age of six months will spread terror in your house, and, hopping all over between table legs and people legs on their skinny cock's feet, will rush to your purse and rip your secrets out with a vengeance, rooting out your identity papers as if they were unearthing worms.

I will make you an enfant terrible, it will be your son and you will not recognize him, your diabolical son.

And as you will be observed by the servants nursemaids valets from the woods—woodsmen, children—all those who do not help you, you won't even be able to crush him like a flea, the slap you strike him very hard won't reach his skinny little detested paw, it will be stopped short on its way. And you will have to content yourself with dealing a swift, sharp cuff to this odious baby's skull, behind the guardians' docile, unfaithful backs.

Your son will engender sons, made for stirring up war. Between us, it will always be a question of life or death. Countless, unrecognizable, the one I'll sow beneath your feet. And you'll never recognize him: that is how you will recognize him.

There is a baby who's been returning for thirty years to wage war on me. But we can't cut to the quick.

Those who are for you a cross, the Queen warns me, those who are for you a renowned cup of poison, I will drag them from the sepulchres of forgetting, and I will seat them, all whitened, at the restaurant table. The old smiles that have lied to you since the time they had all their teeth will shamelessly smile at you at night, as though age had not deprived them of their teeth.

—I'm warning you, says my Queen, what is over grows back.

Expect the musty kiss of those you shall never kiss again. Expect the worst, if it's the truth you'll get it. Expect the truth. Expect the marvelous, ferocious foreignness of truth. Expect to see known and unknown passersby, painted according to your heart's truth. The person time struck in your heart, you will meet her struck with age.

If you want the best, you will get it. Expect the best mixed with the worst. For if you want the freedom I offer you, you cannot have merely half of it. If you are afraid, turn on the light and go home.

If not, come, I will give you all at once: ecstasy and disgust on the same plate, in the same day. We are inseparable.

—Ah! no, I won't turn on the light. Would I refuse my life in freedom? My life plus? The land of my greatest strength? Would I refuse my mystery and my madness?

Would I renounce the land of violence that is pleasure unbound? And all is violent. All is inclined toward incandescence: insignificance glows red and stupidity glows green. I don't know who gave me Night's chance, what divine, demoniac kinship, kindness without prudence and without timidity. But I cannot renounce the night. She is my power and my infirmity: without Her what would I be? A mane without a horse. The copy by my clumsy hand of a picture I will never paint. A woman's regret. A mortal lady, without animals, without nails in my body, without horror, without interest, without screams.

Of course, the night costs me dearly. She makes fun of me. I wander sometimes for weeks in and out of tobacco shops, before altogether ordinary kosher restaurants, I buy olives, and nothing happens. Of course, sometimes I bury myself for a long time in boredom. Night after night I bore myself. I am immersed in the anecdotal.

But that's nothing. Danger is everywhere. I never know what awaits me, what infamy, what brusque exhibition of baseness. The roads and squares might, they do suddenly fill up with war victims, the camp of calamity pours out, a young, mutilated crowd presses forth, pity and horror spread at the sight of these young amputees who cry woe, famine, dance, dance, dance, and then suddenly it is a mêlée, the survivors attack us, a mania for sex wants to eat us, dance us, throw us to the ground, and the struggle begins on this generalized battlefield, where one fights in the name of suffering and cruelty.

If I hadn't wanted to cross this Night, nothing would have happened. But I want to cross. I advance toward the middle of the dream. I could be attacked by a towering blind man. A truly blind man who sees me clearly, it is *me* he seeks, like a blind strength seeking strength. He attacks me. He is taller, stronger, crazier, more unfettered than I.

And it could happen that I exit the battlefield carrying, plastered from my chest to the bottom of my pale dress, an enormous trail of sperm, like the insignia of the order of the gravely wounded. And now, quick, a faucet.

Yes, the night costs me much more than dearly. At night, nothing and no one sleep anymore. Passions, wounds, scars, men, women, children, everything is awake. It is indeed the Bible and its rocks.

But it is also by passing through the Bible and its rocks that I can reascend from dangers to dolor, on all fours in the mud, up to happiness, up to the unique, unnamed taste of happiness.

She has just come, gone, this person for whom I'm headed. My blood retreats and follows her. Myself I am not (following) you, my love, I am leaving you, I am letting you go so as to refind you presently in the lands of forbidden joys, more heartrending still.

Of what consequence are exiles, insignificances, losses, provided the Night accords me a much more illuminating glow than does broad daylight. How I love and how I hate! so high so low so heartrending, I did not know, I do not know, it is She who teaches me.

It is She who ripens the joy barely born of an embrace

into a blaze of tenderness. We who crush tenderness in our precipitation, we who pounce on love with the brutality of hunger. We who look at ourselves in the bright light of day, light that extinguishes the frail, sparkling secrets . . .

I was in a dream with the person I love, where were we, in what bed, we didn't know anymore, in each other's arms, held and kissed, there was neither time nor place, we were in the thickness of joy, until time came to interrupt us, right in the tenderest moment, for it is always so. One cannot forget such tenderness. And then, all night long, dozens of the most distant dreams accumulate atop the sole dream that supports our lives, more and more hostile and even frightening dreams. But if I manage to redescend the Universe, passing through foreign cities, countrysides crammed full with thick heads of corn heaped up like bones, and along the oceans' shore, I end up finding the furtive room, where I once was with this tenderness in the moist, delicious heart of happiness, one inside the other nourished in the dark, ephemeral hollow of the forbidden. What I taste: the infinite taste of the infinite. We were there. Forever are we there, like the ineffable, strong scent of the flower we once were.

This hollow we have hollowed out in memory is crammed full now with scented absence. The forbidden reveals itself. I remember: you were sleeping. Motionless I lifted your slumber and I carried your sleeping body across the centuries. A tiny deity of fired clay. Inside, dreams are fired. I carried your absence in your presence. Like an entire city sleeping inside a stone. Your power in the clay vase. I was at a riverbank, centuries in my arms. Reticent happiness, so as not to interrupt the magnificent absence. Where were you? I took pleasure from this answerless instant. A chaste purity. An acquiescence. The miracle: I needed all the silence in the world so as to hear her breathe. An instant of a familiarity so intense, it becomes strange.

What's going on? I recognized you. It was you. The dream was a salute to eternity. There was a window. The street, the morning, the trees, everything was watching me. Like this body with its centuries and this face that surprised me very gently. A little more. As if I had forgotten what I didn't forget, and all of a sudden it remembered me.

I say: It's you, like an answer, not even a question. And immediately the past renews ties with the future. The years light up. Ah yes, this is happiness: the bread of time. It's tomorrow. The tomorrow that, sleeping, you resembled. And, sleeping, you didn't know it, you didn't give it, you were it. Happiness is having the bread of tomorrow. Today is given me by tomorrow.

And for me Night who is the guardian land of lost lands is also the land of arriving lands.

She is the time that arrives and doesn't fail. The tomorrow who awaits me and plays with me.

Without Her—I cannot imagine a without Her. My strongest strength is in the Night. Night is my author's head of hair. Everything finds, at night, its poem.

Life of my life. Truth of my days that from afar I perceive burning, burning, at the stroke of midnight. I am Hers. I give her all I have, I kill my oxen and I distribute them, I kiss my mother and my daughter and the people who are all I have, and I follow her. Leaving, leaving. Translating my whole life into this foreign tongue, where the words, the same words as here, shine with a secret. Over there, at the Queen's, I am in the secrets, I pleasure everything. Moreover, there I understand that we can take pleasure in everything: pain, happiness, all is joy. The darkest emotions, the nastinesses, the pigsties, all in the end is good.

I see my desired Queen, who from afar flings at me the flash of her revelation, I approach, all is so luminous, I'll be able to read what is written, and when I am very near she burns out. This is how my flight, my betrayal come to an end. Night burns out. I am lost. I am saved. I am delivered into the hands of Waking.

At dawn between the worlds I lose the magic. Barely am I cast onto the shore, the sun not yet visible, soaked, my eyes still closed to this world, my gaze attached like fingers to my departing homeland, with a blind, clumsy pen I jot down in big trembling words: I don't yet know how to walk in this world, and I take unsteady steps. Yesterday upon waking I painted in mournful haste the retreating landscape. And what a landscape! Simple, foreign, and yet majestic: the summit of the prophetic hill is of a marvelous banality. One would think it a camel's back. The close-cropped coat, the thorny tufts, I have known all that. In truth God wants neither draperies nor golden tapestries; it is we who want scenery to help increase our imagination.

It was, then, a bit of dry earth, bathed in a burning solitude. And there—rolled up, tucked away so as to escape the wind's gales—I slept in the corner of a rock. The wind blows on the slumber that I was. In the slumber, in the interior burned a dream's lamp. I saw I was dreaming. Someone woke me, I don't know if it was the wind or the dream. And there, upon waking, I seize the leaf of paper that is always by my side, my paper companion, and between two dreams I jot down: what? The beginning of a magnificent revelation. "Fulfilled, the wind having borne her away," I wrote. It's all there: the secret and the explanation.

The world was returning, my loved ones were arriving, those of the everyday. My daughter came, then a Japanese teacher, then a journalist, then a specialist of Ancient History. I played my parts distractedly, obliquely. Too absorbed in the need to jot down, to jot down these secrets that come from me and that I do not understand. Impoliteness? Well, yes. I could say I am dead, I am absent, I am, in this very moment, seated near a scorched rock on the Horeb; they wouldn't listen to me. Oh well, neither would I. I don't listen. My gaze is turned toward the leaf of paper on which I've written: "Fulfilled. . . ." She is still alive. I see her features, her song's flow, but I no longer hear her. What does that mean? I wonder, and I already call her "that," she who, just a bit ago, was the angel revealed. Phrase, don't go, I cry, mute, to the already departed angel, and I feel the time that nonetheless does not exist, that has neither body nor absence, I feel the time of waking, the time of this world, separate me from the illumination. Time is but: separation. "Fulfilled, the wind having borne her away." The phrase before me, closed. I knew, I lived. I fell from the rock onto this side. One calls this spoliation "existing." But the door remains. There it is, with the magic words. I have the secret's name, but I do not have the strength. I have a lost secret. That's something. I look at the phrase with veneration. It is not the phrase's fault if I do not hear her.[3] She speaks. It is I who no longer see her light. She pales. She is now no more than an angel's imprint.

I await the next departure. I will go forth with my stormy body and my flags of ephemeral splendor and the door will open. Between two revelations I exist, I do my homework. If I must accuse myself, it is of being borne away with the wind. And fulfilled. A freedom I do not have hurls me at full force beyond my walls. Is it my prayer she obeys?[4] Nonetheless, all I have in this world is nostalgia for the magic. The magic is on the other side. I am the submissive, willing object of the terrible Queen.

Why do I feel the need to avow the other life?

Need that began with this book. Need mixed up with the need to write this book, even before I knew what the author was going to write. But there was a direction. And I received this direction like an order, a summons come from the depths, as indisputable as will be the summons of my death. She will say to me: Come, it is time. And I will go. When the author wanted to write this book, the indisputable voice said: go toward truth. A path we've never taken. Not that the author has taken paths contrary to the truth. Writing doesn't lie. But she can tell of so many other things, by distancing herself from the author, and even by approaching the author. And she can circle the truth. The Truth has borders? She has a center? A cupboard? A heart? Yes, in a way. "Go on," said the voice one does not disobey. "Go straight ahead."

The author started on her way, straight ahead. Right away, it looks to me as if some twists and turns have appeared. But that is the author's drama.

As for me, in order to go straight ahead I proceed by avowals. I wrench a door off. I lay a card down on the table. I show my devil. I proclaim my Queen. All this causes me pain. If truth were measured by the violence of the battle, I would deserve it. If by the outcome, I don't know. I write my avowals with severity. Rewriting I cross out, I correct, endlessly I rectify digressions, I drive the lamb brutally, like an ass, straight to the pyre. Up above, on the branches, I tell myself, under the awful searchlight, we will see whom I kill and who I am killed. It will be a demon that will make me shake with shame, I imagine its sex, its sorcery, the ascension breaks my heart. It will be at the very least an enormous bitch with a young dog hanging from her belly spurring her on, being of two beings galloping into the sea. I arrive. I reread. And it isn't true. And yet I wrote this whole chapter hanging from the Truth.

The truth is, I was expecting something else. Carnage, even. But maybe the truth is that there is carnage and I do not see the bodies? And this is the punishment . . .

Privation of punishment?

What have I not avowed?

I hurl myself to the bottom of the depths, into the corner, and I weep, I weep, I weep, which is a form of hopefulness. Ah! my friends, I weep, my friends, if I have hurt someone, forgive me, don't forgive me, warn me, that I may kneel and expiate, and take pleasure in expiating. Especially when it is a woman, and one I love, I weep. Because I should never hurt a woman. Hurting a woman is the worst injury I could inflict on myself. It's as if I had struck my mother. The idea of such a scene is beyond my strengths. In order to express this idea, I've already been obliged to leave humanity. With one leap I return, shivering, to humanity. I don't want to leave here anymore. It's over there that I'd go mad!

We mustn't touch the ax. The ax is mad, she kills whoever touches her.[5]

In truth I've avowed my biggest fault: it is the life I give myself when all the world's asleep except me. But before the cock's first crow, I return, I go down to the kitchen, I prepare breakfast, which is my sacrifice on the altar, and I ask forgiveness in silence to all those I left on the edge of the clock, while I ran around black Asia. Preceded by a shriek of birds, the cock crows: I am already at the table in the circle of debt. I pour the coffee without staining anyone. The bread passes. I am the mother. I am the daughter. I am the sister. I pass from one to the other in turn. We love each other. Do we lie to each other? We rely on each other. We feed each other. I am a woman. Seated at my place, without wings, without banners, without hatred, I find I look like a baguette. I mean to say: a wand of white bread. An edible wand: the magic is in the dough. How moving is life without the Queen. And each thing is of an ancient importance. I have returned.

Self-Portraits of a Blind Woman

Meanwhile the author . . . the author doesn't return. She is all given over to her drama, always.

Why do I speak of the author as if she were not me? Because she isn't me. She departs from me and goes where I don't want to go. Often I sense she is my enemy. Not a hostile enemy, but one who overflows me, disconcerts me, goes so far as to trick me, fleece me, trip me, and display a face I don't approve of. Without doing it on purpose. Ungovernable. Freed. But so as to fall into other prisons from those I am accustomed to. Sometimes all we form is an almost. That would be too easy. Often she is as if dead while *I* live. And conversely. Would I say she crosses me? I suspect her of betraying my affections a bit. But I try not to cross her. Whereas I, since February 12 of this year, have been trying with all my might to seize some brief glimmers of truth, or at least I do all I can to lie as little as possible, the author is preoccupied only with this story. To be told. An ideal story. She sets out . . . so slowly that in the meantime I could tell ten stories. I write under the ground, she says, like a beast, burrowing into the silence of my breast. It is such a suffering. An old story wanting to be told. But look: it is itself opposed. Because in some way it is a burial story. Well, what if the author were to exhume it?

It is as if someone said to us: your dead father, would you like it if he weren't? I cannot look the answer in the face.

One difference between the author and me: the author is the daughter of the dead fathers. *I*'m on the side of my living mother. Between us everything is different, unequal, rending.

How will it end? What is truest on this Thursday in July is that the author doesn't know. The end of the year will come. And there has never been such obscurity before us. Time's womb is pregnant with an unforeseeable brood. We'll see. The horsemen's identity is still unknown. At the end of the year a wall will have been torn down. The plague will have ravaged a house and killed all the cattle. A book will have been written. What will we see? Perhaps the author will have ended up writing the ideal story in this book. This book will tell other stories, too. A story always tells another story. We paint someone's portrait, and it is the portrait of someone else.

The author is afraid. Even so, there are already some notes, a sketch of this Story, I've just read them. All that's needed is to conquer this fear.

The author: When I write a book, there is, under the book's rock, the book I didn't write. When I write a book, I am constantly in the process of not writing another book, I move forward by driving backward, on the banks of each chapter that is born lie, helpless, the pages that have expired, ah! I make my way ferociously, I kill under me, with an intolerable injustice, what I was going to write suddenly slips into the abyss, with one hand I drive back the hand that is held out to me, with the other hand I seize another: this is how I delay the narrative I want so much to write. There will be dead narratives around this narrative, and perhaps this very narrative will not survive a narrative that, in the instant I lean over the paper to decipher the beloved's face, will seize the place I'd like to save.

In me there is an unknown force that writes before me, against me, and that I dread this time more than ever. It is she who is my death.

The solution? To write by surprise. To jot everything down in flashes. To telegraph. To go faster than death. And far from this book whose fields she haunts.

And all of a sudden one day, without warning, to plant this narrative in its improvised state, unfinished but a good likeness, fully into the earth of this text, like a living flag.

How far must one go sometimes to approach a character as inaccessible as desired? To paint the portrait of Macabea,[1] Clarice Lispector went so far as to no longer shave, to no longer wash for six days; then she waited weeks, in a torment that seemed forever unable to come to Term, may she arrive, may the hour arrive, the hour for hurling oneself into the fire, or into the sea, the hour for hurling oneself outside of oneself, but the hour didn't arrive, didn't arrive. "What's this all about?" the author wondered (the he-she one, the one who no longer drank, no longer smoked, no longer played soccer). Her strengths were waning, her author's strengths. By page 24, the author hadn't managed, it hadn't started by page 40, the author wondered if he-she shouldn't go faster, but what was taking place between him the author and her Clarice Lispector who had had to distance herself from himself to the point of depriving herself of male masturbation, they couldn't do anything more about it, shouldn't I, they said to themselves, since the beginning hasn't presented itself, sketch an ending right away, before it's too late? For one could also have imagined (this is what Clarice imagined) that the book was going to write itself before Macabea, for whom it had been fashioned in haste, ever got there. Then it would resemble an uninhabited grave. A boat run aground. An empty museum where our Rodrigo paced before a wall where one could see the dark spot where a painting no longer was.[2] And while they were waiting, apprehension wrote itself, the encounter that roams without alighting. What is going to become of me? The author dimmed. Less and less light— less of me: of her, of him? No one could say anymore. No, it isn't easy to write when the person we invite is extremely foreign to us. We can go so far as to reach those zones of burning dryness where the saints who invited God as a character are suffocating, for in order to find the tongue of God, one must pass through atrocious silences. In order to adjust herself to Macabea's dimness, Clarice Lispector had had to strip herself almost to the bone—beard, fingernails, breath, some ripped-up old clothes, that's all. And the typewriter.

They wouldn't agree to see anyone anymore. The author had the character under her skin, in her hair, in her trembling lassitude, her gumless teeth, I said under her skin, but more precisely, it was under the skin of his skin. A sort of birth of manhood wasn't finding form. The hour didn't come. Arrived the hour for renouncing. Clarice Lispector could no longer wait. She-he was almost dead. Another two months, no more. She-he dragged herself to the bathroom to shave. In the mirror: a horror show. Dark circles under her eyes. At that moment Macabea passed by, and instantly, with the power of a cat, she threw herself on top of her, and, as one commits suicide, in a few flashing pages she seized her, photographed, sketched, and in extremis painted her, sharp and plain. This is how the portrait was painted, when it was too late, too late, at the very second when the too late started. In the end the story was told in urgency, for there were only a few days left. Besides, Macabea's whole life had been but ephemeral. That's why Clarice Lispector had had such a hard time: because a book was too much, a book of an ordinary weight: she had been obliged to consume it down to the very rare measure of Macabea. Half the text was ash. The rest released the very bright glimmer of a flash that was this character's whole life. In the end the book was a good likeness. But in order for a book to be a good likeness, the author has to be one first. When the hour of Macabea arrived at last, Clarice Lispector hadn't been herself for quite some time. This is what the story wanted. The author did the impossible. So well that when we lean very low over the character, who is the only, sickly star this extenuated sky was able to expectorate, this person we see clumsily disposed on the ground at the street corner seems equally to be Clarice Lispector. The two, mother and daughter, mother who went so far as to be father, daughter who lived from nothing but who nonetheless felt loved, by no one, by no one of her acquaintance, the two entangled, resting. It must be said that there had never been room in the terribly meager sky of this story for more than one person. And each one of these two women had been a little less than one so there would be room for two at a time. They kissed, December 9, 1977.[3]

But who was this Rodrigo? He was Clarice's impotence. Her author's incompetence at painting a character stronger than herself, more than herself, because less than herself, character more dying than herself. It was necessary, out of need for this Macabea, for her, Clarice Lispector, to dabble in death. So afraid was she that she began with this fear. She sent Rodrigo as a scout incapable of such sacrifice. He, dreaming of ripe wheat, at the moment when Macabea was making an attempt at survival. And everything took place beyond their strengths. Anguish united them. Death was the victory of their common efforts. Alone, the author had thought she would never make it.

This is how far an author can go, in order to obey a book.

I tell this story poorly, the story of the book in which Clarice Lispector found her death, because I am still alive. Book written from the point of view of death. With death in view. I read it from the other side, there where it has left me. Setting out again toward its mystery. She threw herself under the book. Or the book threw itself on top of her. We have a hard time untangling the bodies.[4]

On the wall near the window, there is, in the author's study, a photo of Clarice Lispector that I do not like. (I am at complete liberty to speak of her because she is dead. The extraordinary liberty that the dead give us, that only the dead give us, is not given to us by the living with whom we live. I can say that I do not like the woman in this photo— without fear. She understands perfectly. We hurt each other in this world out of fear of hurting and of being hurt. Past the door, love, offense, are no longer what we think. And if we could conduct ourselves among ourselves like the dead, it would be Paradise anew. This is what the characters in *The Ideal Story* attempt to do. And this attempt is one of the reasons why the author has a hard time writing: the characters live as though after death.)

As always, Clarice Lispector watches mistrustfully. She doesn't look at us. She doesn't let herself be looked at. She is not the Jewish Bride.[5] Haloed by a white fire, she faces the other toward whom she flows, mistrusting and misbe-trothed. The other toward whom she turns the solar disk of her mistrust, her hair on fire, her gaze of an unseizable color, it is she, coming from the last hour. *Who will I have been?* That's the title of this photo.

There are also photos of Marina Tsvetaeva. One can

look at them without fear. This young woman is not scared. This torrential soul is clothed in a body that is without mistrust. There are no drapes on these photos, no clothing. This woman goes straight ahead. Without precaution. Her body is naked. The windows are open. We see the rocks, the waves, the skin. She is incredibly athletic. A naive soldier. We see the struggle. To be, simply to be Tsvetaeva. This woman is naked. Nakedness is a strength. But what is most naked is her face. It is turned toward us, here it is. It responds. It doesn't attack. Why would it cast a glance at us, when it breathes no fear? We see her naked cheeks. Tranquillity of a woman with all her goods within herself. Her eyes are wide. She doesn't hide the fact that she doesn't see us: she opens her nearsightedness to us. We enter. Inside, it is extremely light. But never light enough to satiate her.

The name of the vision of this woman is, obviously, Intrepidity. She was born naked, open, without walls. That is what renders her so foreign to us. We are not this naked at home.

The author: I need to speak of these women in me who have entered, they have struck me, they have hurt me, in me they have wakened the dead, they have cleared paths, they have brought me wars, gardens, children, foreign families, graveless mournings, and I've tasted the world in their tongues.

They have lived their lives in me. They have written. They have died. They continue unceasingly to live, unceasingly to die, unceasingly to write.

I didn't meet them in the open air. I'm not going to complain: we meet otherwise in the other world, more nakedly; we bear the blows better. And we need the blows that only the dead strike us. And if I had met them? That wouldn't have stopped me from reading them far from them.

And why Clarice, why Marina? Why not those near to me, why not you, why not thou? It is forbidden. I cannot say of what is woven the imperceptible cage we live in, and that is us.

I cannot say we live there where proximity turns to separation. Because I don't even know.

Between us, where is the truth? She is between us. She is this tangle of blows and caresses that I cannot even contemplate without dread. Already I shudder. Who strikes who is struck, between mother and daughter, between me and you, between people who are bound to each other?

I fear my sister's truth like the butcher shop.

I'm afraid to see the thorax of the slaughtered ox, glowing in my penumbra.[6] Its viscera frighten me, I'm afraid to see the entrails of our thoughts. The motionless red and yellow of truth.

I cannot say, I cannot tell. If by chance I happened one day to catch a glimpse, through an accidental tear, of an image of what occurs between us, I would be terrified.

No, I cannot speak of you who are too much me. I'm afraid of the blows. Might I say the resentment that accompanies tenderness? The wishes for punishment? The absolute dispossession? The gaze that turns away in horror from the face of the beloved? I cannot speak of myself. I'm afraid that if I said, *I* have never raised a hand against any of my children, my daughter would burst out laughing. One doesn't see one's own hand rise.

There are those one cherishes with whom one speaks the least, less and less, in whom one confides less and less, and one ends up no longer saying or loving anything, thinking behind one's back, talking to oneself, but not to the other, telling oneself everything bad about the other, but not to the other,

And this is how one loves one's daughter, one's son, one's brother, one's sister, one's friend, one swallows everything at once, and it's love, bitter love

And how many times does what takes place between us resemble a tragedy?

In act 1 the person who loves us asks us to die. She doesn't say to us: die. It's worse. She asks: give me your blood, give me your second helpings, give me your liquids, give me your marrows. It gets worse: this is why we love this person, because she needs so much to eat us. We are the bread, the air, the restfulness, the boat, we lift her, we lay her down, she sucks us down to the marrow, we are God, we are no longer me, we are no longer very far from extinction, the mountain has been gnawed down to the core. For all these reasons, we have for the person we love a love gnawed down to the core. It gets worse. Because in fairy tales, the child kills the ogre, we are the child and we are not the ogre, in fairy tales we know perfectly well with what side of the ax we are sliced, and we take pleasure in the clarity. But in grown-up fairy tales, Serguei asks Marina: give me your blood, give me your milk, give me your sweat, give me children, give me your hours, give me your poems, asks blind, innocent, urgent—who will extinguish this extinction? When it's the child who is the ogre, there is no good side, Marina is herself author of the ogre, and she trembles twenty years for her frail, thirsty days. It gets worse. From what does she feed herself during the famine? From feebleness, from phantoms, from her own sublimated marrows. Between him and me, thinks the mother obscurely, I choose him in spite of me. It is not I who choose, it is life, that kingdom of ogres. Besides, the ogres have changed. We used to love that old fool King Lear. Today, we've grown up. We have an athletic body, the little ogre is diaphanous. But it gets still worse . . . what happens in our house, we cannot say. It's too dark in here for me to be able to paint the true. It is within this obscurity that life prospers. I should complain?

In my mother's room there are several photos of the author. The author is smiling broadly, baring all her teeth. I detest these photos. I am convinced they never look like me.

The author is a complex open milieu composed of other planets. A strange attractor. Zone of relative instability in which a population enters, enters and exits, enters and exits, goes away, and returns. Enter Clarice Lispector, then recedes, one revolution, and Clarice returns. Always here, sometimes at a very great distance—but she has become as necessary as Omi my grandmother. What relationship to Omi? It's a matter of roots, I think. Of the love of roots. Of old women. I think . . .

Sometimes the author can go so far as to thrust aside her friends, her bodies, her books, as one thrusts aside a sheet, a roof, one's strongest and most authoritarian inhabitants, but the repulsion is part of the attraction, and those thrust aside end up returning.

Enter and exit Clarice, enter Marina, then recedes, one revolution, Clarice returns, recedes, enter a very dear friend, then recedes, one revolution, and sometimes, all of them have exited, sometimes just one has returned, sometimes, in the incalculable game of our diverse revolutions, all of them have returned, there are interradiances, sometimes musical entanglements, modification is constant, slight, the sky wavers. I lie in wait. Enter and exit one of them, then returns and exits once, will return? returns once, doesn't return, will not return? Perhaps she was just passing through? So be it. Forgotten? Then the following year, returns.

In me radiate women I wouldn't even love in the open air, but in the mystery, I love them beyond love. What do I love . . . ?

What relationship between a Clarice, a Marina, a

Rembrandt, an . . , a Thomas, an . . . ? I search, for weeks, I suffer, I am in the state of the mathematician who's going to find, behind him ignorance conquered, before him ignorance to be conquered, and if he does not find he is dead, he is only an imminence, an expiring ear, a prayer to no God, he is in his bath, his body is in the bath his head searches for the solution, his searching head flies over sands, sciences, thinks, thinks, his body weighs, weighs, descends heavily, flows, and suddenly, finds! It is the body in the bath that finds what one need never search too far for.

And what do I find? I find: *the ax,* I find: *the dream.* I find: *the worst.*

These are three names for the same light.

Ah I see it clearly, I love them because they have said: *the worst.* To say the worst is such a great joy. But once said, we can no longer stay.

That is what happened the day when Angela Pralini, the woman who was Clarice that year, 1976, said to Eduardo—the man she had learned to love and who had taught her the courage and the joy to be this Angela, for Eduardo, the philosophy professor who, despite philosophy and through her [philosophy], had metamorphosed her into a woman—what she had learned to think of him.[7] That same evening she took the train at Central Station. It was beautiful, what she thought of him, but it was the worst. Because it was almost exactly the truth. She had looked at Eduardo, she had seen him. Upon which she needed to tell Eduardo what she saw. This isn't done. This is what Clarice, in her wily need that is a way of loving thoughtfully, always avoids doing, leaving to her Angela the worry and the risk of doing what one shouldn't do. So Angela, having looked at her Eduardo whom she loved, needed to tell him: that she was not he, and not like him; she lover of music and of Dostoyevsky's novels, he no such lover. She lover of the long, penetrating smell of the forest, and of the heavy weight of animals, and he guarding against loving what does not speak. She loving passionately, in advance, and still after being dead, her lover Eduardo, loving him skin, flesh, blood, viscera, bones, loving him with the scent of rotting leaves, loving him with nipples held out like a baby's hands, with her uterus quivering, she loving him down to her bones, loving him beneath the phrases, returning to her newborn's wailings, loving him on the sly, worming her way beneath his lectures behind his papers, back to the prehistoric era, in feverish furtiveness adoring him, adoring his genius, loving his need to be loved, loving him as he was, with, as a mirror, the prettified world of big-city society, as he was a very handsome man without eternity, her lover Eduardo suffering from sicknesses of the soul, with ingenuity, as if they had been invented for him: the sicknesses, the terror, and the soul. And death also. It is him she needed to tell one Tuesday, to tell that she loved him so much—he whose guilt occupied space similarly to an enormous dog defending its master, threatening to bite anyone who would try to tell Eduardo that he didn't need to be defended by such a ferocious guilt. She who for ten years hadn't needed to say, suddenly one Tuesday, she adored him naked, as he is: it was, by the way, by the very light of truth that she loved him. This is love: loving the other for his fatalities. But she also loved the truth, to which she suddenly needed to make a declaration.

Because perfect love, she thought, is fed from imperfections. As for her, Angela, she was only imperfections. Suffering sometimes from jealousy, or worse: from wounded vanity. Which made her suffer in her pride.

So this Tuesday was irresistible and without ulterior motive: like a sneeze. All of a sudden she leapt to the other side of love: to the side where one loves and says all. She loved loving in this new, exalted, aggressive way. She loved tasting the pleasure of saying aloud what in ten years' time she had never heard herself say. Pleasure in war. Without calculation. She emerged from him. And, from outside, she sent him violent love rays. She had made it to this day of necessity. Unforeseeable day, which can arrive or never arrive. There are women who die before an imperative day happens to them. But not Angela. Still young, and there it was.

And saying what she thought even if it isn't any more true than what he thought. Because my truth is a truth limited by the truth that flanks and surpasses it.

So it was for the pleasure of saying something that she alone thought, and perhaps for the pleasure of committing an act, or making a blunder, or a sacrifice, or more precisely out of a need to not forbid herself from saying any old thing, one sole time. It was as though she had declared her own strangeness flamboyant.

She said: there can even be deception in love, and even disapprobation. And even boredom. And why did she say all that, like one opens a window. Outside, the salty smell of the air. Not so as to tell the truth that does not exist plainly. But so as to be refined: so as to try not to lie. Merely not to lie. This was a day of great naïveté, useless but necessary. The need for strangeness was satisfied. For untangling.

So she left. She took the train. At Central Station. The hour of truth was in the train. A truth limited—to itself—a half-truth. That's how Clarice seeks the truth: as far as to err, as far as to stray.

In the train, Angela was nowhere: between departure and arrival, between dying and reviving. What she accomplished was one of our worst secrets: in the very heart of our intimacy our personal solitude grows. She was in the process of realizing an instant of fidelity to our human solitude. See why Clarice needs Angela, and I need this Clarice:

so as to dare to declare solitude. And even in the other's arms, it strikes us. This doesn't stop us from needing the arms that separate us.

"The worst"? This is what we call what at our age has become forbidden for us not to forget. Because in childhood we would bathe happily in what will be the worst. Without disgust. But next we learn to forget so as to be able to "see" as we should, our childhood squares become modern diamonds, and we are disgusted. It is clear from photos that they've never put their eyelids on. They do not smile at us.

They live at the level of dreams. In broad daylight by the light of dreams. A light that we can only bear at night, when we're sure that it's a dream. It is clear from the very first words: a dry, cutting wind blows. Ah yes, immediately they cut our anchors. What they want is beyond the temperate night, which we live off during the day.

The author has almost finished writing *The Ideal Story.* The end is only a matter of a few lines, a decision. At that moment everything stops. The child cannot be born, does not want to be born. We were stunned at having forgotten a child. What is forgotten? the child in the room next door? How can one forget-expect a baby? Forget to bring it to term? Well, it can happen, it has already happened to the author. It has happened in several lives and several dreams. To many women. This is our most forgotten secret. A forgetting stronger than waking robs her of what she has just accomplished. Ah! forgetting an infant—this can only happen to a mother, and it is an experience from which she definitively carries the frightening scar, and then, her whole life she seeks to forget this forgetting, but the stigmata is unforgettable.

Was it forgetting that befell Marina Tsvetaeva as well in 1919? in 1920? And in the middle of a conversation with Alya, her own daughter, behold: she receives such a stroke of present memory! I completely forgot Irina. The other daughter. I ran through the streets, I climbed the moonless stairs, I carried the sack of potatoes on my back, I burned the piano legs, whom must I have forgotten? Irina. Forgetting's baby. Has not been fed. For? Two days? It is time that has fallen down the moonless stairway. Stopped, I no longer move. The idea of going to find the dead child is unfaceable. The face of the dead baby, our hunger, our forgetting. And all the poems I won't have fed, won't have saved. Yet I wrote them. Instead of running, I am stopped. The worst brings out the worst. Until the humble blood that *must,* begins again to flow. I go there as one goes to the house of the dead. As one descends to take one's place in Hell. Deprived of the pain her death would cause me if she hadn't died of my forgetting. I go there, wholly dead, wholly dead. Into the room next door so far so far from my heart. And I enter.

I, too, have forgotten a child in the room next door. When I remembered, ten years later, my mother no longer knew where the tomb was buried. This can happen to us.

But what is characteristic of the author's baby is that, once forgotten, it will end up returning to her in memory. This doesn't affect the forgetting. The forgetting is absolutely pure. Barely written, struck with forgetting. Kidnapped. In the baby's place, forgetting: a silent formless thickness. The painless pain that comes to close the unreal door to dreams. The weight of the tomb of dreams. Forgotten dreams are our forgotten children. In the same way the author suffers in this moment from an indefinable absence, phantom suffering for a ghost. All she feels is a vague irritation. A tomb weighs like a hand on her chest. And she struggles for another breath. It is still the hour of forgetting. She moves with difficulty. Forgetting is the invisible master of space.

I shall continue to paint this woman's portrait. Everything starts to happen to her inside her mother's breast before her birth. During this time her mother speaks to her in German, and she calls her Alexander. Her mother was expecting an Alex/*ander*. The other.[8] The éclat of this prenatality stays with Marina. To have been what she was not. To have him. And then she wasn't he. It is this story of the unexpected. We expect Alexander. And she is: the other. So it will be: her: him: *ander:* he on the other side. The other side of her.

(During this time the author searches desperately for the names of the characters in *The Ideal Story*. What to call them? If she could, all would be saved. She would shout out their names. But perhaps this story takes place without names? Beneath names?)

Marina provokes this Alexander, she looks for him, she doesn't flee him, she defies him, she defends Marina, she cannot be Alexander, she cannot cease having carried this name, having heard the voice of love call her by this name, and all is entangled entangled, love, nonlove, the name, life. Who am I, who must I be, by dint of seeking she finds, at the age of four, Alexander is in the library, it is Pushkin and it is she. He is standing before her, *Complete Works,* heavy, golden, fleshy, she turns him upside down, crawls on him, spells him word by word. She makes love with this book, with this Alexander, who is so there, so heavy, who tells her stories. And all these stories she suckles from, it is Alexander who invented them and so it is she. At five years old she has already eaten *Complete Works,* she has drunk them all, they are hers. She is full of them, she is pierced by blows, rocked, marked, charmed, incurable. She is born from his *Works.* Pushkin is her mother tongue, he is her mother. And still more than mother because this Pushkin gives her all at once. At the same time as life, language, his magic words, his stories, his children, and his women, she receives his death. In the room. It takes place on the wall, before Marina's eyes. His death: the death of all poets. The bullet struck the belly. Hit Pushkin's belly.[9] From this belly she is revived. This is a difficult story to tell because there is no breach between what is in the book and what is in the room: what is written happens to Marina in reality. Alexander's book merely has a head start. And she, always ahead, ahead by a life, by a birth, by a separation, since she has already read, lived, lost, enjoyed everything, on the one hand already written, already dead, but on the other not at all, on the other not yet, on the other, woman, lover, greedy, not yet knowing anything of what she already knows. What has been is to be. With emotion she waits for the story to become flesh: the magic must be constantly demonstrated. She runs the world over; the thing that comes to her from the most faraway place in the tempest's troubled tumult, this unknown thing, it can only be, she thinks, filled with desire, filled with fear, the best-known thing. What transports her with joy is the troubled time that flows between the thing and her. The time when we do not know yet and already, when we are going to love whom we already love, and we have such a short time for enjoying our blindness. As long as this troubled time lasts, she is happy, the thing approaches. It is life itself. Instantly the unknown will end, and it will be death. The bullet has left the chamber.

Nothing stops love, the thing, the race of the unknown one toward we who race toward her.

Let's enter the tempest. We see her go toward love, in that direction, is it a wolf? is it a tree? as one goes toward the sea, with big intrepid steps, loving ahead without knowing if the sea will be there, but there she goes. The sea isn't there. Not on this side. "I was sure you wouldn't be there!" she cries. In the instant she says it it's true, but not before. Before she is five years old, thirty-seven years old and she's running.

The most important thing is to go. For years she sets out, she moves toward the encounter, with this love she attacks living things and dead things and the dying things that are the poets, ahead and after, she is going to love them, the bullet has left, it flies. It aims, it hits the belly, of women, seeking the women promised by Pushkin, announced by Rimbaud, the women up ahead. The sugar of life. But unfortunately in that time there were even fewer women than poets. It doesn't matter.

Just because no one is there yet doesn't mean we shouldn't love.

She loves the women
from after her death.

Sometimes we find her seated on a bench. She's expecting him. How could he arrive (he, Pushkin), since he died in that room? That's why she's expecting him. He can come some other way. In a dream. She believes in dreams. It's in reality that the end arrives.

She is awakened on May 3, 1926. Some approaching thing is coming through the distances, coming from Val-Mont through Glion sur Territet (Vaud) Switzerland, that which is going to strike her momentarily, at that very hour in May, is Rilke. His name in person. And his full address.

Strike her with flapping wings, through the very distances, *mit Fernen, mit Flügelschlägen,* with flapping *f*'s. At thirty-four years old, barely awake, still flying from one side to the other, on the edge, of night, of waking, it is on this edge, in the troubled blue of the sky, that it moves toward her, the thing that is Rilke, still living and already flying from one side to the other, on the edge.

It is on awakening that we ask her what this thing that's coming and toward which she goes is called, the word, it is at the door to dreaming that she utters it, and the thing comes, came, still comes in her dreams. In the blue space that stretches, blurry, before her eyes. It is always a matter of this entanglement of the unknown with the known that is life itself. Ah! let's not stop coming, and going, *und dann und wann, kommt der ihn trägt dem der ihn trug, entgegen,* to the encounter, bringing ourselves the encounter, giving ourselves the comings and goings, the most beautiful instants in the world, let's not stop not yet having arrived. And each centimeter of the universe quivers between us. Marina gets up, it is six o'clock in the morning on May 9, 1926, and, seizing the distances, she dashes straight into the outburst, coming from Saint-Gilles-sur-Vie, coming from Vendée, coming from France, coming from her strange homeland/sur/vival, at a speed that delights in slowness, for she is the self-consuming flash, she becomes the Angel of the Nonencounter. What delights me is this slow speed, this potency in impotence from which we may only obtain pleasure on the streets of our dreams.

Provided, she travels, that the best-known thing, the hoped-for, remains unknown to me for a long time. Thinking already and forever about the bullet, about the belly, and working with all the strengths of her slowness, to hold back fate, almost strangling the horses, protecting herself from the arrival, wearing herself out at burning each step, a little more than alive and half dead and without saying so, and in 1926, thanks to her the distance has never been so deep, so vast, it is a world, and above shines the Encounter, in the farthest corner in the most troubled part of the cloudy sky.

And all this, this carnal resistance to threatening happiness, this ardent, twisted, necessary emigration, for nothing.

As if she didn't feel coming the ultimate foreignness that's now speaking its unheard-of language in Rilke, and murmuring messages to him from the King of Aulnes. They're calling to him there in the back, don't you hear? Not hear how he unknows himself from hour to hour; and he loses himself in his own garden where tall roses he didn't plant himself grow. Neither plant, nor prune, nor water, unknown roses of a pale pink color, straight, like arrows, and young, and which are, don't you see, messengers of his death. Here, at the edge of his own garden, grows a poem he did not write. In him grows an unknown vegetation that disavows him and whose elegance and rigidity he cannot deny.

But she, Marina, doesn't sense it coming, believing it is always from herself that danger proceeds. And altogether busy defending her chance, she doesn't see that her efforts are in vain. The nonencounter has already promised in a low voice that it will come to the other end of distance, with golden raiments and unknown games for Rainer Maria.

Marina paints her self-portrait:

"The books I love most in the world, those with which I will be burned: *The Niebelungen, The Iliad, The Sayings of the Ost of Igor.*"

First she prophesies. Then she executes. Fire awaits her, awaits the books she loves. What she loves: promised to the fire. She loves what is promised to the fire.

She will die of books. In the fire of books. With a book

of fire one can inflame her. There is no difference between reading, writing, burning, loving, dying rekindling. Fire is her future. She who was born from a poet's belly.

She is fed with flames, glutted with filters. We cannot know if those she loves have destroyed or constructed the world. She is in the same circle, in the enceinte. "And from all sides love, love, love." She means to say: fire, fire, ash. She knows all the degrees of fire, all the colors, all the tongues. She is born: fire. And that is what she promises, violently, to whoever approaches her, to whoever deserves and doesn't flee the approach of her incredibly athletic soul. Honestly: come, I will take you in my arms of flame.

What she loves: the books in which she revives as other. Your book? The supreme degree. My bed become clouds.

The cloud inflames December 1927. One never knows, when one is metamorphosis, who burns whom. The fire, the fire.

She burns, she doesn't lie. With what does she feed the fire? With books, with letters, with whatever comes along, with her breaths with her visions, with her poems. The fire wants fast fast fast. It's going to die. Another letter. The last. No more letters? No one to write a letter to. They've all gone. The fire dies.

———————

And all this, it is the name *Alexander* that wanted it. The name that ends in—*ash*.[10]

In the belly of the room there is a book in whose belly there is a man in whose belly there is the music in whose flow the child finds joy and drowning, in whose belly all the way at the bottom, a body metamorphoses into verse—light on its feet, into songs of coral and precious stones. Everything that surrounds Marina is in Marina.

Inside Marina, there is Maria, but this is not yet known. Marina sleeps in the belly of the storyteller. What is sweet about the song is that it sings three stories at once. *Push* means featherbed in Russian but *push* also means cannon, there is between Push-Kin an upsetting movement, flight and fall, life and death carry the same caressing name, feathers, cannon, together and conversely.

A man is called Rainer Maria Rilke. Half the work is done. All the world hears . . . what. Hears. Each of us according to our ears, according to our tongue, our memory, according to our hunger, our despair.

In advance he is: poem. Poems are: something inside names that makes us think we hear the thing that isn't said. From however far away she thinks she hears him, he promises Marina: church, childhood, chivalry. A man is called Maria. From her, Maria, Marina expects everything. From Rainer: nothing at all. In advance letter by letter in her, is he.

But Clarice told a story without names. She was walking the other morning on Ipanema beach at the still nonhuman hour, nude at the hour for nudity, walking so as to walk alongside the Ocean, with the Ocean; it was the hour when a woman likes to walk accompanied by the world. The woman becomes immense, calm, powerful, the ocean becomes tender, immense, discreet. It is the ideal.

But: from the far side of the sands came a man, running, rushed, she sees him come toward her, busy, he wants the time, that's all she had on her, on her wrist. She without interrupting her walk with the Ocean, he comes abreast of her, a young man, well built, and in his simple round blue eyes the question: —but she didn't have the time to tell him the time. —Are you looking for a man? asked the young man. For one second she thought: Has someone found a man? Has a man been found? Lost over there in the sands? Do I look like I've lost my man? Right away she said: —Are you the man? —Yes, the man said simply. —No, thank you, she said, I have what I need. —For whatever you'd like, he said. For going out. Or simply a restaurant. No, thank you, she said. Like a doe the man returned to the prehuman sands. All lightness. And she continued her walk, she with the ocean. And he? He, she thought, without woman. Are you the man? Yes, I am the man. Clarice saw that she had in truth just seen a man, simply a man. Man unknowing of good and evil. Man and One, obviously. And looking for a woman, as it is written. Never had anyone asked her for a woman so simply: man points out to God that he is one, and that he is missing the other. For doing whatever you'd like. The important thing is to be able to walk with. He thinks: a man looks for a woman; so and in the same way a woman is: she who looks for a man.

Because a man is not made to be alone, but so that God may place a woman by his side. And never had Clarice been so simple. The man had come straight out of the sands of innocence.

And she? she lied: I have what I need. She was unable to say anything and unable to do anything except lie to so much innocence. Because the man dated from a very ancient era, forgotten long ago by her and even forgotten forever. But books existed. This morning I saw man, she thought, moved. Without a name. Without trouble, without tumult, without tempest. Looking, naturally. And she, before his blue eyes, she was a woman, obviously: he mistaken by the nudity that made her seem like "a woman." She thought: it was really man, before names. We recognize him by his organs. A simplicity she had already lost forever, she who was often "sought" for her invisible secrets. And she herself didn't know by what name to designate the person she loved. It wasn't man, and it wasn't woman, thousands of years' worth of images, characters come from every book, every country, all their generations, thousands of photographs, thousands of unknown, now-known things complicated their two persons so infinitely, they could no longer just simply love each other before words, but—to the contrary, after, from the other side; by throwing themselves into the ocean from the tops of mountains of thoughts. She who went on a world tour in order to be with the ocean. She thought with uneasy emotion of the man: a survivor. A species she had thought extinct. There are still some, way over there.

She is called Clarice Lispector, how could this flash of comprehension followed immediately by a flash of incomprehension not follow.

I didn't foresee telling this story. But I sensed it had its place in this book.

In order to tell a certain story, sometimes we must tell another story, and go so far as to burn it. We don't do this on purpose. We want to go to the Rose. On the way we meet the *lonza*.[11] In order to ascend, we begin by descending. We cross paths with Virgil. How not to let ourselves be led? And thus from canto to canto we ramble, from fascination to forgetting, this is how we get to the Rose, inversely.

But isn't everyone going there? Some, believing they're on their way, turn their backs on it and so never get there. Will the author make it inversely to the Rose? I do everything, absolutely everything in my power for this. For the moment, the author goes from contretemps to contretemps. I have nothing against contretemps. I adore the *Inferno*. But how could I read it if I didn't know in advance that Dante won't let himself be turned away at the last minute from Paradise?

And in the same way the author who wants to write *The Ideal Story* in fact just wrote the *Story of a Contretemps*. She felt obliged. (Not to worry too quickly. It's medicine.) As long as she ends up at the Rose. It is often novels that trick us with contretemps: take *La Duchesse de Langeais*. In one of the first chapters the author locks us up for fifty pages as far away as possible from what interests us. And next we have the impression of having escaped the sepulchre.

Take *The Gambler* by Dostoyevsky: enough to make one give up hope, right?

And in one of his last books, Thomas B. makes an appointment with us at the Museum of Ancient Art. He has something to tell us, he tells us. We're there. In the Museum for one hundred pages. You must be wondering why I summoned you here, he tells us on page 130. There is a reason, but I'll tell it to you later, later. I don't know *how* I'm going to tell you this reason . . . later . . . later.

This is it: a real book! I recognize it by its gasping. One doesn't know *how*. The guests are here, the readers. One entertains them. One has something essential to say to them; later, later, one is getting to it, one will get to it at the first possible page. Finally on page 218, at last, one invites them to go to the theater. What, was that it, the essential? Naturally at the theater they're doing that strange marvel *The Broken Jug*.[12] That brittle comedy. But isn't it already page 216? Do we still have time to go and break us a jug? —Excuse me, says our author, I've made you come all this way for this, it's ridiculous. —For what? For the theater? — For writing . . . these 218 pages. I didn't do it on purpose: it's only now that I begin to suspect myself . . . . My intention was to invite you to the theater.

So that was the reason. The real but hidden reason for which he made us come to the Museum. And there told of lives, deaths, friendships, disgusts, while waiting for later.

And for hours, that is to say for years, he or it (the author, the book?) didn't manage to tell us the "truth." Not knowing if it was a matter of going to the theater, or of going up to page 218. The stage is not where we think it is. We're not reading the book we think we're reading, and in order to see *The Broken Jug* must we spend 218 pages in the Museum? We go there quickly. Page 218. It's late. Must we go there? We no longer have the time to think—and we're on page 219. It's the end. We've made it there. The Jug is broken. Broken twice. It was an abominable production. We should leave before the end, but there's no more time, it's the end of the book. This doesn't matter to us. It's too late for regrets.

—In the meantime, we could have gone three times around the world.

—Haven't we? Together, and without knowing it. So we go: around the world. There where we do not know that we are led. No one knows.

Our guide doesn't know where he's going. That's why I love Thomas B., because of the force with which he guides us *elsewhere*. In his books, it seems to be a matter of museums, of cafés, of constructions, destructions, hospitals. In the end it is only a matter (of writing), (of preparations for writing), (of dying of writing). Seen from up close, writing is an awful fight. You're going to make it. We're expecting you. Someone takes hold of your body by strength of arms, and immediately: a fight to the death. It is writing in all its forms that attacks him. Once it's an eighty-two-year-old man who grabs him, a toothless man who won't let go. Sometimes a young woman, often a young woman, always a Persian, stops him, retains him. As soon as the author settles into a huge, empty, never-before-lived-in house, there he is, the shameless old man, the persecutor. Since you're here, I'll invite myself, he says. From room to room one flees him. I'm leaving at Easter, we lie, thinking we'll mislead him.

And unfortunately this becomes the truth: at Easter, there we are, fleeing. On our tracks the book suffers. We don't write it, we counterwrite it, we toss it onto the paper. But up to the last chapter we still hope to write it ourselves, and, bent over it, we congratulate ourselves for having *saved* it. In the end it is only a matter of preparations that last until the grave.

I'm coming, I'm coming, says the author. Tomorrow, tomorrow all will be over, says the gambler.

She was in the process of writing her Ideal Story. Instead of continuing . . , she turns back fifty pages. And see, another contretemps. A nothing detours her. A question. And it's a whole story. As if what we want are the things that do not happen to us. Not in reality. Let's sit down.

Because this *Story of Contretemps* begins with *a bench*. I recognize it: indeed, it is the one where Pushkin breaks it off with his Tatiana. The one before which Marina, a hundred years later, stops, struck with expectation. Under the influence of this story.

But in truth the story started with the race in the garden. We hear the horse arriving. All is coming from extremely far away. Who has fled before he arrives? Onegin. Someone the author (Pushkin) doesn't like much, knowing him. Tatiana escapes straight to the garden, she runs, she flies, not daring to look back, not daring to see that he isn't following her, she's expecting the one she flees, the arbor of clipped hornbeam, the footbridge, the meadow, the garden path, the little wood, breaking lilac branches, the stream, the flowers, and out of breath on the bench, she falls. One can't flee any farther. Hope stops here. Fear. The bench, the stream. On the other side, pain starts.

What I love: the race, what Marina loves: the bench. Each one reads in her own book. The author: hesitates. In Marina's: a bench.

A bench. On the bench Tatiana. Enter Onegin. He doesn't sit down. Everything is already broken off. It is she who gets up. Reparation? They remain standing, the two of them. Separation. All two of them. But it's only he who speaks. He speaks for a long time. All the time. *She* doesn't say a word. Between them, speech doesn't give the word.

Time, long time, distancing has entered: with large strokes between the two of them he digs and digs: "I was not born for happiness, my soul is foreign to it. Marriage would kill us. Loving you from too close, very quickly I would grow accustomed and love would cease. If I were to love, it would be from afar, from time to time, separately."

Marina reads. This is love, the story tells her: a bench, and between *she* who is on the bench and *he* who enters, *he* and *she* in the halo of isolating italics.

. . . But before the bench, the race. And before the race: the letter. Tatiana's letter. She writes: "This was decreed from above: it is heaven's will. I am *thine.* . . ." She says *thou* to *him,* she says *thou* to the one who will arrive, who's going to arrive, who arrives, to the stranger who is *him,* it is indeed *him,* and see how it is she who, hearing him come from the end of time, bends her bow, and says: *Thou. Thou,* the violent Thou, with which I thee and thou God, because I do not know him, with which I order him to exist, and *He* is *him.*

She says to *him: Thou!* And in her first letter to her *him,* Marina says *Thou* to Rilke, *Du,* she suddenly addresses him as *thou,* in German, in *his* tongue, which for her is her foreign tongue, the tongue where she moves toward him, she flies, she aims, Rainer Maria Rilke! she calls him and rejects him (she loves him).

Tatiana's letter is always before us: "I am thine. It is heaven's will." It is one letter too much. Come from too much, from too high, from too far and too soon, departed much too soon,

That's love, says the Story: a matter of the letter that left too soon. It is a matter of the letter's hour. Time of departure, time of arrival. The arrow departs from one life and aims at the other. It is a matter of the juxtaposition of two stories, it is a matter of the two of us, one seated, the other standing, between us God knows how many bobbins. The letter leaves, it cannot not leave. It is heaven's will. Which isn't familiar with our clocks.

It is the letter's Author who is writing this story, our story. The Letter goes everywhere, too fast, too soon, too late, the foreigner who addresses us as Thou and hurts us. That's love: the letter that never arrives according to our time, that arrives according to some foreign time.

It's always a matter of a story: you can change the names, the address. Enter the Duchess of Langeais. And one instant too soon Armand de Montriveau. Or else one instant too late. The escape begins, and we don't know who's pursuing whom, in what direction, toward the Orient, toward the Occident, or if we're going toward Africa, our heroic mother, or if we're moving away from her, or toward the flesh of Egypt, eternal meat, or toward Catholic fasting, toward the forbidden, toward famine escorted by the music of angels. We play with the sea. It rises, it recedes, we miss the tide. And death rips the bread from our mouths. What am I saying? No. It is we who have refused the bread, the spices, the refreshments.

And the letter? Yes, there is always a letter. She had cast him a letter. Alas, it is the one that doesn't arrive: for in this letter is the time. The hour is. The limit. She gave him one hour. Believing, naturally, that she was giving him all. But we cannot arrive on time. That doesn't happen. You who love us must give us everything. Not even the time: everything, nothing, yes. The waiting of the mother who waits no more, who has given us everything, every departure. Who has given us what we would like to have: absence, presence, return, more, never, I don't know. It is only thus, inside the infinite space that watches us without impatience, that lets us abandon it, that we will return.

And the title that Balzac did not give his story is: *Don't touch the ax*. Because in the end he didn't know anymore who the ax was. We begin telling a story so as to return a blow, but in the end, while we've been writing the ax has turned on us. This is not our fault, neither hers nor his. The ax is. The hour. The story starts before us.

We are always too young when it starts. We still have glassy, dark-blue eyes. We, imperious nurslings, claim until the age of forty, then until fifty, and then until even later, that love must be according to our time. This is our hope, our innocence, and our source of torment, we who are claimants and wooers.

Time differences are native, they are human differences, we don't want to admit it. Luckily, for we who are mortal, we don't admit it. Otherwise, we would never go to love.

Story that we hate and love to read. This is the mystery. Could it be that we love to read the stories we hate?

To what extent we need death cannot be expressed. How we call to her with our terrified wishes, we beg her not to come, in what horror we adore her, no, this we do not express. Unless she crosses our path, we're unhappy. And how to express the ferocity we name love. And the number of times when we attack the adversary we love, we struggle and we are conquered together. We live backward: this is a penchant that cannot be expressed.

It is secret. It is so secret that it cannot even be expressed in English, in French. . . .

This story, I cried, I have heard it enough. It is an error, a beautiful wickedness. Each time the letter doesn't arrive, Tristan turns to the wall and I weep. I don't want this. The hour—the wall—the ax. Yes, we love to weep. But only in books. Not in life. In reality we don't like death, we only like her shadow, her footstep in the garden, to hear the ax breathing above our bed.

We love to play at death: this is our unknown crime. The one that cannot be expressed.

The misfortune is that authors need to commit this crime: I am in the process of approaching the truth. Be careful, because when it is ready to explode, it will vanish on the spot.

I advance: Shakespeare cannot not write love by the light of the ax, cannot not write the letter that arrives *too* soon, too late, and never according to its proper time, because: writing is itself the spirit of contretemps. While Cleopatra and Antony are in an embrace, plunged in a now of flesh, in a sole mouth, their two souls entangled, there isn't much to say. She (writing) merely awaits their separation: that is her kingdom.

I accuse writing of being the author . . . of

. . . I lost the truth, as I feared I would. That means I had actually found it.

It is dark under my earth. I am a little lost. Perhaps I've said what I meant to say. If I could retrace my pages and read myself. But in such a darkness I can only write by following myself, all the way to the end. I am now in the dark part of truth.

131

I don't know yet how far the author will have to go in order to obey this book. Where are we going? This book has already changed titles several times. A title appears. Three days later another. And to think the author has only written books without titles up until now, and without panic. A book can only name itself at the end, naturally: so it seems to me. But see how this one names itself constantly. There is an endless trying on. *Rembrandt's Deaths; Lives; Deaths; My Deaths; A Revelation;* or else it might be called: *To Truth.* Which would be an indication. A prayer. One could hope. "To Truth," mute goddess to whom we address all our dissimulations in the hope she will dispel them.

Such a quantity of titles is a sign of distress. One might think: the Slaughtered Ox trying on hats. Without a doubt, there is a child suffering inside the mother. The mother crawls under the earth, the child inside the mother. How far will we go?

Sometimes we have to go so far as to throw ourselves into the Dead Sea.

Although I didn't want to do it, I did it. I was under the author's influence.

Decked out, adorned, what were we doing at this hour, my mother and I, on this huge empty square that is called, perhaps, the Pantheon, white as a bone, sunny, picturesque? We were wasting time, we were moving further from our goal. Anxious about the hour, the whiteness, I emerged from time, seeking the hope of a taxi. But in the burnt horizon of this deserted Paris, nothing. Apparently we were in Paris. Might there be a bus? A lady tells us there is. When? Over there. I want to get off at the New York, Algeria stop, I say. Yes, fine. The stop is over there, invisible. A tall man, unnoticed until now, accompanies us to the other side. We have to climb a curving slope that ends in several vertical meters. And still no music, not a note.

Reading Dante is an endless labor that moves us further from our goal at the same rate as we move forward. That is what we were doing in reality. In Dante, philosophy and poetry are always at work. Even the stop is like a reserved élan, a staircase landing where conversation is conquered by an alpine exploit. I cross the last few meters with a bound. Then, once I've made it onto a narrow path, I don't know how, I hoist my mother up. Say, is this amount of relief normal for such an esplanade? Or is this the esplanade at Invalides?

Once up there, no metaphors. "We have time," says the man. And see how he leads us in our descent to the other side toward a big, white, water basin, insisting, by means of rigorous verbal attacks: it will do you good to bathe in immortality, we'll drink, we'll take a dip, we've all done it—such pressure that finally I am *obliged* to let myself, descend the slope, I am *obliged* to do what I do not want to do and advise myself against doing, *obliged* by all these words, by the obligation coming from these words, from this insistence, imagine a monument of words raised to the glory of the word *immortality* that had no consistency, I surrendered, obliged, I decided to put only my foot in it, which is already a risk, and, in effect, still accompanied by the song of this man who was extolling to me the Dead Sea in which he's already washing himself like a little bird, all the same I end up wading in all the way up to the roots of my hair. . . . Well then, from now on for all time I will let myself be obliged unto death by spoken words, only this man the spoken words, a man come over from the Pantheon in order to get mixed up, in the end, in my life's conduct? Like lightning shattering a cloud of salt, abruptly, I emerged. I escaped. I broke through the crust. It was the first bath of my life in the Dead Sea! I emerged from it with a bound, still young, dissatisfied, wet, salty, but safe. I retraced my steps, running, with my mother, leaving behind us the Immortals, croaking like frogs, immersed in the basin.

Why did I have such an absurd dream, endlessly opposing myself to my own will, and obeying this imitation of death, without any desire, out of pure *obligation,* and always further, lower, closer to my nothingness, but then suddenly I got myself out of it. I indicated my disagreement. My disenchantment,

All this because—now I'm going to make a capital revelation—the author thinks she cannot go to Jerusalem. The author thinks: "The author cannot go to Jerusalem." There. I've told the secret. There's no going back. Everything's here, and each word is a part of everything. There is "the author," there is Jerusalem. And between the two the idea: an impossibility. The impossibility binds them. The impossibility of going to Jerusalem exists so strongly. And is so strong. It is one of the author's strengths. One might say it is a weakness. But such an intense, insistent, haunting weakness can only be a strength.

The impossibility of going to Jerusalem, and for that matter anywhere near that City, and by contagion to Israel, is the door before which events, books, "things" have brought the author year after year until this year.

And for this very reason the author thinks about it. She even seems to be obliged to head in the direction of Jerusalem. In her notebooks I found hundreds of pages on the *J* motif. One might think sometimes that J. is her aim, but that's not it. I think J. is her theme: J.'s impossibility.

For the author it is a matter of one of those impossibilities we hold as dear as we do our own head. Impossibility for Thomas B. not to have been born in Austria, impossibility to have been born there, him, Thomas B. A birth that looks out onto death. And his entire life he shakes this earth, his mortal land, as if he could, by ripping off his skin, uproot it, he austriches the entire earth, he goes all the way to Palma, and it's still Vienna.

And for the author, impossibility of going to Jerusalem, to the lost land, impossibility of renouncing wanting to go there. As if she couldn't go there without her father. And yet she wishes to remain faithful to her father's desire.

What irritates me is that it is not her desire at all. It is not my desire, or my impossibility.

—But it's an obligatory desire: one cannot imagine anything more tyrannical, more distressing than an obligatory desire, thinks the author.

Who thinks inside me? Who wants inside us? So it is for Marina: she shouldn't have let herself be written by Pushkin. Unfortunately, he is in her.

The author:

And unfortunately for me, I must still do battle against my dead. Last night I was in a white horror: I dreamed I was unable to dream the dream that would deliver me. And that all night long I was running, motionless, after the dream of dreams. It's a matter of finding my dead and taking them where I want. There is something insurmountable. How to depart with my eighty dead when I cannot see them? They're here, in this bus, I assert. I boast of having gotten them in here. And now I am going to drive them where I want. Where? To J. But nothing moves. One cannot force them. No force in the world. The dead are much stronger than we. My exhaustion is infinite. I couldn't even dream my own dream. Me in a dream before the door to a dream in which my dead were locked up, inaccessible to my prayers and to my will.

———————

Enough! The Ideal Story now, I cried.

—Tomorrow, tomorrow, the author tells me. I cannot write without them yet, she begs me. One more day! The last!

But I, emerging from death with a bound, already salty but saved, I cry: No! No! It's over! No more tomorrow! Today!

—One more hour! The time it takes to get to Jerusalem.

—To Jerusalem? Ah! no. Then let's split up right here.

—Wait, wait, listen, the author tells me. Maybe, I suddenly tell myself today, a Wednesday, maybe all this traveling that's been preoccupying my brain and making a world—wandered over and over, tiredly and tirelessly, out of my interior space—maybe this inexhaustible and thus marvelous tension of my motionless being planted there in my existence J-ward, is but the exterior, geographical, magnificent figure of this other strangely impossible action—that I call: writing books. Of this marvelous, terrible action that is but hope and can hope for nothing but hoping. Can neither hope nor win, nor come to an end, nor reach, nor arrive.

So I must go there, she prayed, in reality, to see to what extent it is impossible to go there. I want to write this: this journey. I want to go to the end of impossibility. I beg you, one more day, one patience, one chapter. I'll write beautiful things that will make you weep. One more step. Are you coming?

I was going to surrender. Was I going to let myself be guided one more time far from myself by this will that leads me ax-ward, and one more time? And continue counterwriting this book in spite of me?

I stopped short on page 200. The stop was so strong, so tense that for several days that's all I could do: stop, be stopped. My blood circulated with great difficulty, crossing my chest, so hard was my heart. Flesh and thought hardened into a no for a whole week. At night I dreamed of any old thing, far from me, far from the author.

136

Such a brutal separation, I never would have thought it possible. After all, isn't the author also me, or at least I thought so? Not so much then. Nothing is impossible. We can even split ourselves from ourselves. No reason to be a slave to this one here.

No, I say, there is no impossibility. That's the truth's sickness. One must merely write books otherwise. Everything is a little more possible than we think. It is our thought that doesn't know how to think more frankly.

We can invent supplementary steps to Hell. Our ingenuity is limitless.

And to get to the Rose? About-face. Nothing simpler. About-face and straight ahead. And above all, no explanation, no discussion: it is through words that death makes its return.

At that moment I look at my watch. It is noon on Wednesday. At noon. It is at this hour that I was able to break up with the author, something unhoped for.

Maybe I will return to her in a few years—or else presently—but I'm not thinking about that right now. I don't even know where she's gone. It is the moment for opening the book to *The Ideal Story*.

Quick! With a bound I rise, I extract the ax, I kill death! I run to the next room where the forgotten child lies helpless. I enter.

The child is here, so sad in its cradle, neglected for weeks. She bends over the unresponsive cradle. And with her voice she knocks on the door to life. Yoo-hoo, my baby! she humbly hopes. All at once there is a miracle. All it takes is to recall it. On the little, faded-rose colored face, the life flow returns. The child smiles broadly, baring all its teeth. Ah, it's mine all right. It wanted to recognize its mother. —From the depths of shattered forgetting, I respond to you—Child's goodness. O immortal creature who is proof even against forgetting. Then the ancient joys return, the old movements. The mother is revived! In her heart resurges love, milk streams. Joyfully she takes up the little one. How good it was once upon a time to take up the child, to feed it, to be fed from it, she remembers. In this present memory she takes it in her hands, with shining clumsiness, and throughout the room flows the pale blood of reviviscence. What are you doing? Aren't you going to run and find some milk? There's some in the kitchen. I'm going I'm going.

I swim inside reality. I'm alive! I am a miracle's chosen one. I enter, I exit, the doors remain open.

Quick! The Present has begun! Yes! I'm coming, quick.

An Ideal Story

Quick! Let's transport ourselves to the café. . . . The two characters—the author has left them without names. I name: I think this story is about Clarice and Isaac.

Let's transport ourselves to the café where Clarice suddenly saw him.

They are seated. It begins with a bench. She speaks without looking at him. They skirt each other, side by side. Next, Isaac speaks. Only about poems, about prison and the poem's freedom. Suddenly their story begins. At this very moment, in the café. They weren't watching each other. Didn't watch each other arrive, didn't see each other. Love declares itself without words. If ever a dark lightning bolt existed, this was it. They are struck. Clarice feels the blow. I didn't ask for this, she says. She looks at the room. She sees the tables, the chairs, but not him. At that moment it was noon. What, could this be love, this astonishment? Around the two of them everything becomes slightly more luminous. A little more than luminous. Except them. They were all dark. She didn't even see, in that instant, to what extent she couldn't see him. A dark stain inside the light. But the voices meet. There the encounter came to pass, inside a growing shyness. Time is extremely slow: it spreads out over years. But inversely so swift that they are rushed far ahead of each thought. Thereupon, on their astonishment, falls the word: *never*.

On all this falls the word *never*: on the café, the chairs, the years to come.

Each one coming from such distanced countries. She loves, he loves, with never. Without country. He says: *Nie*. And *never* becomes *nest* in another tongue.[1]

He gives her never. She didn't know it was: the present. An infinite never that doesn't know the time. Starting with *Nie* she learns. It is an art, an address, it is a calling: the study of love, without the help of death.

Everything begins with this "never," inside of which there are times. A desert with gardens. A very dry paradise.

The proffered hand forthwith recovered, forthwith restored, but restored lost. There is no hope. That is their secret.

Leaving the café, still giddy from the blow, standing, but overturned by the invisible cart, she noticed she hadn't seen Isaac. She had remained interior, her voice close to his voice. Next time, I'm going to look at him. But years later she still had never done so. They would always meet each other interiorly. Their bodies have come to know each other, body to body, but without images. She is exceptionally tall, something I immediately forget. For I see her mingled with the air and sea, her elements.

Next the story lasts for a very long time. They watch it pass with equal astonishment, decade after decade.

(I'm trying to write without death. Will this be a tragedy? I do not know. I am: following them. This slightly strange story gets stranger and stranger as, gradually, outside, years pass. So fragile and so eternal. . . ?)

They live like two extremely free prisoners. Giving each other the extraordinary freedom the dead give us. Traveling, writing, meeting, inside separation. In its heart, in its parenthesis arms.

They loved this sort of life they hadn't wanted: without any property, without a house, without a roof, life in the desert with a jug and two baskets, see what has befallen them from the sky: other life. Other than their lives.

Unable to decide anything, they received. By blows, by surprise. Time in the garden: there's some, almost none, but enough. A little time, just enough. In-between time, hanging from invisible gold threads all over the earth.

And for country: distance. There is a country between us. *Es ist ein Land Distanz,* woven of echoes and Voices. There is a country Distance: echoes in the body, echoes in space. Between us the far, a little more and a little less.

And for earth: absences, absences with presence, absences without forgetting, with evocation

Without earths, without roof, but never without text. That is the secret.

Is it a knack? I do not know. Sometimes we may think they don't belong to the human genre; that would be a mistake. Those who know them bear witness: they are like you and me. Only struck once upon a time, a long time ago, overturned, and rushed: into a story. That didn't die of death. As if punished with happiness. Excuse me, I'm painting clumsily, because, I must avow it right here, I feel in loving them a great repulsion. As much "author" as I am, and apt at a certain asceticism, I won't go so far as to "understand" an inhuman condition.

I who feel a hidden ecstasy in sharing a meal with the beloved. We eat the bread of the world and all is forgiven.

Something our characters never do. To such an extent that they never shared a daily meal: the few rare times they happened to take a meal together, they ate in the silent light with modesty. As if they had been raised together at the breast. And then never again. As if they had never eaten together again since the breast. But slowly recovering that most ancient of tastes.

I follow them: there was no country. But there was a place that grew up around them. There was always a book for covering each other. Between them, long letters they didn't post, didn't send each other, sent each other otherwise.

And correspondence? There is none. A direct letter, directly, she can't envisage. This would be a rupture of the infinite. She can't resolve herself to it. *The* letter, they were writing it, there was only one, it was this unending story.

They spoke the same language: it is of her that I would like to speak. A very rapid language, in which they had met and loved each other before loving each other: heard and understood each other. Their winged, elliptical tongue, which they could speak with the same luminous swiftness in their other tongues.

In their tongue, where they encounter no limits. Taking pleasure one before the other in all-powerfulness: they went along, with the calm immodesty that increases strength tenfold, eagerly pursuing thoughts much stronger than themselves. A writing aloud. This is what they permitted themselves to do. In the forest, eyes closed, seeking the unheard-of.

This is why, whenever they speak to each other the beautiful darkness that gathers them together, they are tense like wild beasts, trembling with alarm, and exiting the expedition, breathless, they lay down on the ground, runners conquered by triumph. Exhaustion that was restful, quiet, and composed: because it was their own exhaustion.

And there were the texts: written in their other tongues, in which they visited each other.

(Without tongues, would this story have been? Without our maternal fatherlands with their movable, scented flesh? They had always lived there. Born to the sorcery of living elsewhere, born to the modern sorcery of speaking to the one who isn't there, nourished with magic words. Born to the difficulty in taking pleasure from absence.)

They would meet in several tongues, going from one tongue to the other, completing one with the other: whatever can't be wept in Brazilian she makes resound in Russian, he, playing with French in his German; and each one adventuring with awkward but hopeful steps into the other's tongues.

They suffer a little, without knowing if from innocence or guilt: never getting used to having become strangers. Strangers among us, falling, rushing, outside all laws, strangers to themselves. They aren't recognizable. This preserves a gleam of infantile astonishment in their eyes—"I can't believe that this woman, who loves what I would not have loved, is me." Violence continues to precede them.

As if they were reading this story (which is theirs) in a book, with the most vivid incredulity.

Because it was a story. And they hadn't had the idea. They had been struck with innocence.

But this doesn't exist, we're not permitted to be innocent, not on earth.

Living under two laws, obeying two legislations, they stumble.

Feeling themselves suddenly guilty of such innocence. So they flee inside a storm. Believing the storm is pursuing them.

Would they be punished for having such luck?

(I, too, as a child, I was uneasy with happiness.)

But they had paid in advance, right? Having been fulfilled and deprived in the same hour, and thrown into the desert. And even so, sometimes they wonder if they aren't still much too rich. But we cannot live from less. The next less is death.

So they permit themselves to take pleasure from their great poverty. Clarice would go to the market on Fridays and before the vegetable stands would take pleasure from absence and solitude, and from the innocent beauty of vegetables. The world has its perfection. We, too, we have the pale, quiet perfection of vegetables.

God, god, god, permit and pardon, never had there been such a secret religion, such religious pleasure.

They call on God, in whom they don't believe, for help, because living so invisibly is sometimes very similar to dying. And God answering them, they returned to their story's intense light.

(I forgot to say: they never called each other by name. Between them no Clarice, no Isaac. There was no staircase down which to call the name, no familial garden path, no balcony. No use. And in the interior, they lived in nameless nakedness.)

Inhabitant, I no longer know what to call you,

most ancient and most young,

save to call you my pain—for this is the most beautiful
*   compliment I can pay you,*

pain that is synonymous with joy, joy

synonymous with pain

What a stranger you are to me, stranger-woman,
*   stranger-man, my*

love,

As I am to myself, and I let myself go

to you till almost, till almost approaching

the never-attained state, never-desired state of
*   appropriation*

How, without attributing you to me, is this "us"

nonetheless formed? "Us," this very

top-secret, vital creation.

Us, *by the way, is the altitude of the mountain*
I permit myself to attain. Saying us *is*
the violence I permit myself in silence, terrifying
us, *that one would only know how to say at the end*
of forty years, our, *the weddingless hourless nuptials,*
And yet we share nothing each
day if not this flesh formed of wordless
thoughts
The vibrating Space of the Between us. The sky is
blues. I meant to say: blues.

I forgot to say: they were nameless, but not voiceless. In this story there is the telephone, like a third heart, common heart, the story's heart.

Without a telephone this story could not have taken place. Without angels with voices and trumpets, would there have been Revelation? There must be voices and trumpets.

I will sing their telephone: it is almost impossible for me to speak of this because I don't know what that place in the body is called, where voices touch, doors open, voices enter, and they march, they advance, they kiss, they have incredibly soft skin, and hands that quiver softly at contact with the soul, I don't know what to call this place where, while making love, there is creation of the body with which the love is made. A place exists into which they descend together thanks to the telephone: passing *directly*, without any transition through the exterior into the heart of the interior. What I know: the absence of exterior. And then the descent. The rest I guess at, at the ends of the lines of Isaac's poems. After the very short lines comes the quiet, wordless part, a silence straining like an ear, and listening: it's that way—over there.

Your ear to my ear, I hear: your ear; I hear: your hearing, I hear your thoughts' breath, it's this way—over here. In the region to where the voices hiding inside the voices descend. They use the telephone like an invisible ladder of dwarfs: in a flash one slips down to the center of the earth. And there: treasures, only treasures.

It is easier for me to speak of what would happen before, and around the telephone. Before calling him, Clarice would prepare herself at length for an hour: a quiet concentration. Carefully gathering up all her last thoughts. Sometimes she would begin the night before. Choosing like a woman: the best of herself, the strongest, the most alarming, the most naked. Dressing so as to undress then dress in nakedness, as we do. Seeking the most precisely becoming translations. The ceremony, different each time, is a labor— never come to the telephone without having prepared. Had she been able to sing. . . . It was almost a song. The phrases that would come enveloped in her voice's flesh were of the hardness of a writing near at hand. She would note: the kernel. The stone on which she constructs a musical temple.

In the moment of the telephone there must be a great silence in the house. This is what she didn't have. Noises in the kitchen: a ripping of flesh. She really could have killed the cook. She killed her. The dog is part of the telephone: it waits. Not everyone can paint or telephone with the same incantation. It was Isaac's love that compelled her. But never has she written of these times. They were of the number of things that come to pass beyond the power of writing, like the moments when, making love, we are like gods who know not what they do.

It was on the telephone that their books found their source. Unpublished source. Much purer source, Clarice would say, than her published books; not regretted. She marveled at the source. Who is author of the poet? "It would be awful if I were myself author of the author that I am." But the author is anonymous; she-he is the genius of the situation. Which accords us the grace to be what we can.

And before the telephone there had been the café. And the "never" that took the visible half of the world from them and, in exchange, gave them the invisible.

It had promised: never, with inside this never always the garden but a sporadic garden. Kept, the promise gave them bizarre riches.

Everything we haven't had together: suitcases, hotels, automobiles, address books, debarkations, we could have had, we had. Together in the interior where the impossible doesn't enter.

But I read all the books with my eyes and your eyes.

All they had from life was luxury: transfiguration. The air where they meet, the beauty of the air where the street, the café is found.

There where they pass together: a slight illumination. The last time it was the first Saturday of the month of May around noon. Near the scaffolding. In the insignificant street. Insignificance in May is this instant's title.

The instant is a miracle of simplicity. Its perfection: meeting each other. We race from the far end of the garden of life at top speed toward *her,* toward *him* and, in the end, instead of not being there, of not receiving the letter, of causing the ax to fly, instead of a not-her, not-him—She-he are here, together. The bench doesn't disunite them. Meeting each other as it no longer happens these days: at the same second, at the same smile. By one second: saved. Trembling from sensing we were saved. We behaved like criminals, like the pursued, we fought with all our might against all the dangers, we cast quick glances all around us like threatened beasts, because with each beat of time we were escaping, from ruin, from death, from execution,

This is why the street was transfigured. It was, in that instant, the last street. The scene of our death. In this formless, charmless, treeless scenery, the scene of our death was being staged inside us.

Irradiation of colors. The light gray of the suit. The light gray of the voice. The pupils so green under the painted eyelids that they shine black. And the calculated dress: equal to an absence of dress.

And also all they did not say to each other. That abundance, those armfuls of thoughts, those roots of eternity, and that afflux, that germination, that overrichness one would like to unburden oneself of. Luxurious epic beneath the marvelous mask of banality. For each of their sentences was marvelously banal. Each utterance hidden by ash. —You have freckles. —For more than thirty years. As though they had stopped before a shoe-shop window. Each prophecy replaced without ceremony. And, barely parted from each other, all this, this brief, light, insignificant dialogue, instantaneously transforms itself into metered verse.

Without offering you my arm, while extending to you my hand.

I scaled thousands of steps, one step away from you.

What was not was the ephemeral, the rootless.

Everything swears, everything hopes, everything counts on the extremely distant alliance.

And the strength of the instant is: believing together, at the same time, in the incredible

And one step away from you I will still scale thousands of steps. (He crossed out steps and put: stairs)

O trennen wir uns	O let's part
noch einmal	again
trennen wir uns	let's part
und schwimmen	and let's swim
wir schwierig	with difficulty
unentwegt	with obstinacy
einander entgegen	one toward the other

During the instant each second writes itself already. In the very instant breathes the instant's future. The first faint lights:

A modest sensation of happiness. Nothing grandiose.

The gathering up in the insignificant instant of a long time made of gasping absence, of expectation.

A transparent bet kept. Both seen from a divine airplane. The miracle: that the miracle is without violence. Street, houses, pavement, faces, hair, everything is a little more. A little stronger, a little more dazzling. As if eternity's floodlight were lighting the scene.

There was a swift, shy, confident, anxious kiss, similar to a first kiss. The delicacy of the first kiss after the resurrection. I knew your lips in another life. Their lips regained a virginity. Our four astonished lips in the dark woods. This one was: the first.

She returned home haloed by the first faint lights of the future. This is how the neighborhood made of insignificances enters the legend. By explosions without violence.

Who are you for me, she wondered, in her somber office, contemplating nonetheless the face of her dog, whom she loves like a son. On the wall behind her, the echo: portrait of herself asking: but who am I? portrait of her astonishment. You as mysterious as my dog, you wordless also, you who never lack for words.

Not her mother he is not her son, not her father, no one from her family, searching all over the house, the family, who, someone very familiar, extremely unknown, the most unknown person in the family: the most familiar unfamiliar thing, the dark thing that draws near inside the tempest's troubled tumult and two minutes later became a man, and two minutes later, became the child-fear, and two minutes later enters in me, in my language, and there, becomes: a woman. A woman? She was surprised. Inside the troubled tumult of language, the dark thing had enveloped her in the tenderness we call woman. One life would not suffice for explaining this mystery.

The things that come to us aboard images of language always cause us to quiver with surprise. We suddenly see what in reality we hadn't seen. Revelation of hidden constellations.

This is why Clarice loved reading poems: so as to better see.

She loves him in the interior. On the exterior she never lingers, only barely when she sees him coming dressed in all his handsomeness. In the interior reign freedom and the humor of dreams.

We have loved each other for such a long time, dozens of years, without reflection, without image, and one day we realize we've come to the heart of the wild forest. It is dark and mild one inside the other, and we don't even know whom we're carrying who is carrying us. Love broods us in the same egg.

Surely this is not a man, she tells herself. In her books

150

men were academics, and, in spite of herself, she devoted a ruinous admiration to them: the more she admired them the smaller they grew, until they became the size of a cigarette. She smoked them. Or else man of an unknown species? Dream-man. All that would subsist of lecture-man were his genitals. At the beach she only had eyes for women, like everybody else. Men being merely an obligation of nature.

And "me"? Such a long life and will I never know what I have been for you, Isaac, what thing, of what color? But this she had learned: she was born to set him free. She was the judge we need to set us free. To give us the freedom of dreams.

But she doesn't prevent him from accusing himself. Because we need to accuse ourselves. She was born to give him the freedom to accuse himself all the way to the extremity of accusation. To give him the great lunar freedom that only the friends who are still faithful to us in death give us: so he can feel assured of judgment and condemnation, and on the other hand assured of pardon and protection. Protected to the point of being able to bear his own condemnation. Because sometimes we need, in order to bear too much luck, to be judged, weighed, and condemned. Isaac suffers from happiness and Clarice was born to give it *back* to him. But not to take it from him, something she regretted a bit, because, despite her strength, she had stayed in close touch with the nervousness of the woman that she was as well. Not having in her the capacity to hurt him (but only because to hurt Isaac was to hurt herself first), she had the regret. She would have liked to be able one time to be a woman who causes crying. It wasn't for lack of desire that she was not so, but for lack of competence.

But at least she tried to imagine:

Could I hurt you? (She hopes. He: No. He: slight compact human body at rest, indistinct from the terrestrial body.)

Could I hurt you? (She hopes: perhaps he didn't understand the question. He: No.)

But I'd like to hurt you, can't you understand this, can't you imagine it, I'd like to wrench sounds of human love from you, love that causes the belly to ache, hunger, cold, agonizing, sweating, burning, blushing, moaning, after the fall.

—No.

—But if I were to disappear? (She hopes at the limit of hope.)

—No.

No, if you disappeared it wouldn't be you, it would be your disappearance that would hurt me.

But you might be able to hurt me. You might be able.

———————

I can't even accuse him of pride, she resigns herself. Only of confidence. But she didn't have within her what it takes to wound this confidence, neither Abraham's sainthood nor the impiety of the woman who isn't afraid to strike the flesh she loves. In vain was she biblical in appearance, especially her face, and above all, so beautiful one might fear her beauty, despite her black eyes that, seen from very close up, were suddenly dark green, and despite her indifferent eyebrows and her mouth—as if it were rejecting the kiss it had inspired—she had the spiteless soul of the New Testament. Nothing to be done. Even as a maiden, even as a child, she was already mother and grandmother and ancestor, even betrayed, nothing to be done. The limit to her happiness: she would never be able to know the dark-green pleasure of great heartrending discord. This was her fault. Because she had no doubt that he was capable of suffering. But it was only some other woman who could offer him those pangs. Which made her rejoice. Since she wasn't armed for assassination's aftermath. So why this desire roaming around in pain? And that she only desires in thought and without body.

Clarice: Because I want everything, I want more.

Listen, you can drink my blood, why wouldn't I drink your blood, says the Virgin, half fainting with horror, which is an intimidated voluptuousness.

I want to go where I cannot go, I want to leap over myself and land on the other side of myself. The truth is *further on*. I want further. Where I'm afraid to go: that's where I want to go. The life I'm seeking is hidden behind the fear. Fortunately, there is fear, its banner red and black, to show me the way.

I want to go as far as to drink my own blood. For this joy is a sword. I hurt myself on you, and I do not say so. Not for ten years. Behind us the long paths of years, blows, and wounds. As far as my ugliness and your ugliness, as far as my crime and your crime I'll go, I have gone, I'll go farther, as far as to wound the dark heart that beats hidden in the sunflower forest, as far as to suffer I go, I'll go, and farther than suffering, as far as to suffer no more.

I hurt myself on you, I hurl myself onto your rocks, I break myself into tragedies, small, but ferocious, but furtive but ferocious, my fate is being played out down below in the huge sun-faded circus, which, seen from here, is no bigger than a shallow dish. A white skull, a pinhead on a die, this is what I am in the eyes of the constellations, I undo myself beneath your feet, I know the pain of all women, I go farther as far as the hallways and curtains of novels, farther and lower, I fall into dust, I efface myself beneath your wheels, with all my might I beat the stony heart inside me and tear lacerating lightning from it, with your help I carve myself up and wrench flames from myself

But from evil and blood are born coral branches and giant flower forests with sunflower songs of praise. That's me there, between the stalks, that animal of a soft beige color, turning its silky stripes to the wind.

And further than loving as far as not to love.

Nothing has happened to me since you that hasn't changed inside my cave into occasions for psalms and ironies.

I make scenes for you, without telling you, I cut passion into two equal parts and I keep all the tears. If you saw in which coffin I cross which streams—but I won't tell you my coffin. Not before having burned it.

A woman needs all her pleasures. I wouldn't want to have not received all the blows that have opened the dark-green eyes in my wall. I need to feel beneath my fingers the fissures and scars that trace the treasure map on the skin of my soul. I explore myself. I terrify myself. I spread without modesty my bloods and my excrements: you will never read what I write.

I inflict the following on myself as well: I write to you with intention. With the intention of aiming at you. You are the target onto which I won't discharge my arrows. Myself the bow drawn from neck to ankles, my muscles are so hard that in the morning I am speckled with bruises, all the violence I address to you accomplishes itself on me. The letter explodes in my chest. In me it is you I torture beneath the wheel. What counts is grazing life's filament, sharp, so sharp, out gush pearls of blood, and having gnawed the bones down to the marrow. When I'm dead they will reconstitute my love for you, starting with my jaw.

There now, it's this Saturday. One of those millennial days that strike us straight off. I'm cold. The word *journey* is leaving, taking with it, in its nets, a catch of stars. The word *journey* empties the city around me. The word *journey* suddenly rhymes with *funerals,* with *hemorrhage,* with *impenetrable.* At the call of the word *journey* a woman bends over a pyre: she reads her future in the flames. At the word *journey* an unknown woman telephones me to announce that she is going away to die, she, too. Tears in my eyes, I forbid her to go.

But before this today I've lived this Saturday the twelfth from top to bottom, hour by hour, I've evoked, undone and redone it, on the eighth I was the eleventh, days crumble into dust, we don't need to climb toward the summit, the mountain itself collapses and melts beneath our feet, and on the tenth it was already almost the twelfth, the little white cloud that is Elie had become a big gray cloud and on the eleventh there was a storm, it was already the twelfth. We can always look for God on days like this: he isn't in our hearts' convulsions, he isn't in the fissures of our dreams. He too has fled.

In God's place I have, as friend to my alarms, both sides of a leaf of paper. Under the hours' whistling, I dream of the mystery of the leaf, my impoverished god. We, too, we are both sides my love, and the back side is the front, and I, too, I am indissociably back and front. When I write I never know what side I'm on, if it's mine or yours, if I'm leaving or if you're leaving in me, if I'm writing on you or if you're writing on me; constantly I twist and turn. Without the leaf of paper to listen to me I couldn't live through this Saturday. Leaf, I love you. Whoever you are and so much more than I. Slight, infinite creature, tricky marvel of nature, an everything that seems like nothing, I write to you beneath the hours' wind. I complain to you and I feel, in complaining to you, a joy of extreme curiosity. Because a world is revealed to me, and in its hoarse and apparently inarticulate rages, by dint of paying attention, I discern a music. All it takes is paying attention, not letting go of the winds the clouds in your head, all it takes is not letting go of the leaf of paper, for visions to emerge from chaos. The little open book is always in the hand of the Angel with the legs of fire, its right foot on the earth its left foot on the sea; we are not forbidden from going forth to grab it. All it takes is not forgetting.

Often I forget, I live without little books; life without the too tall Angel is more comfortable. But you with your Saturdays and your departures you send me rip-roaring storms to shake me up.

From the depths of time climbs the familiar alarm, the enemy, the cry of the boat in the tempest. Trumpets! Paper! Ready? The eyelids fall. I've seen thousands of departures: each time it is the same surgery performed with flint. The cosmos is chopped up and boned. The heavy sky descends heavily onto the earth and crushes its chest—my muddy, suffocated chest. Moon and sun extinguished; the earth is flat: a directionless road. The three-year-old child draws near its end: it begins here, beneath its naked feet, with its yellow bricks going nowhere, the end of the once animated world. From between its knees the crouching child watches the dirty yellow ground of abandon go creeping by. If it were a boy, the child would be stretched out on his back and, with atrociously silent eyes, he would watch the dirty yellow nothingness unfurl. But it's a girl. Above her back the sky has turned to earth. An ancestral solitude entwines me and sweeps me under the floor to Saturday, down to the basement of maternal seas, the home of the drowned.

This horror, truthfully, I'm telling you, today I want to flee it, I want to exit from the boiling oil, but in three days I'll be able to remember it.

Never will departure's black magic be all used up.

I've studied the farewell: it can't be learned. It is our imperceptible master. We lie the words of good-bye, we swallow them like medicines, and we never know what despair, what bitter mistrust they hold, mingled with the thirst for believing. Good-bye tastes like aloes. Good-bye, the hour says to us. What! Is this death? Well yes, it must be lived.

I detest nostalgia, and I love its name so much. Black and red poem, nuptials of aloes. A taste for the little open book. It seems that in order to find the honey, one must chew Liliaceae leaves. Nostalgia is almah, the Arab dancing girl. She tells me stories of the drowned, the deadest of this world's dead. Nostalgia wants to drown us. I miss you as though I had died before you. And dead I remain here, I see you, I hear you, you don't hear me. That is the greatest torment. One lives oneself as dead. Or else it's you. On one side you, on the other me. One dead, the other alive, irrecoverably.

Already I was born so as to see my mother die. We crossed paths. I should have never been reborn. Never will the black diamond abandon be all used up.

In my dreams you become malicious. The air around you is dark. You sit in the dark and you do not move. The one who sits is a vision of mute repulsion. He isn't open, he doesn't shine. He attracts me in order to repel me. I circle him weakly, humiliated firefly, I would like at least to throw myself into the fire: this is forbidden. Between us: the insurmountable; there is nothing more horrible: the wall is inside the heart. Between us is hostility: love turned to poison. In vain I attempt to say a word. Seated in front of him I say, like someone who doesn't want to drown:

—Where will you be next week? —In Europe, he says. —In Europe? where in Europe?

—In Europe.

I am profoundly shocked. To not even tell me in which country! This is how far the malice I strike you with in my dreams can go. As far as to exile me and exile you. A tongue of flames emerges from my mouth. As for him, when he asks me where I'm going, I'll tell him: to Europe. And I'll make him drink the ironic potion of malice. He is in front of me, I would never have believed it. I am the dream's excess. I look all around me: who constructed this dream? Who wrote this bitter little book? Who painted you without the slightest light, so as to wound and threaten me? Who announces to me the desert, the forgetting, the uprooting? I seek, wounded, I seek, whoever paints the worst

I saw a horror film about you, Isaac, and I don't know who made it. In this film you were your opposite and I was my opposite.

Ah, now I understand where I've been. I've been to the devil. I'm going to tell you: I was so afraid of this Saturday, Isaac, that I went all the way to the devil. Hell was right here. You said to me: go to the devil. And you were the devil. The devil is an impassive man. He sits. He is closed in on himself. No one can die for him, or run to him, either from joy or from pain. Never will I forget this sight.

You give me black and white. For thirty years we have been watching each other leave, smiling, only your eyes and my eyes, only our four eyes, the gray ones and the green. All of a sudden a foreign eye came to me, an eye without éclat, an evil eye. We think we are superhuman, we brag about ourselves. At noon one Saturday, see what we've become: objects of time, tiny bones. Gods we don't even know play at making us leap into the air in order to then land on the backs of their hands. Truly we are nothings. And without explanation.

—Careful! Don't let us fall! Airplanes, automobiles, memories, foreign cities, careful! Here we are returned to our natural truth, we are tiny bones, fragments of a past humanity, flung this Saturday into the air of chance. I crouch, I watch the world come to an end, and I weep.

"Today I feel like weeping."

I've just jotted down this sentence. This desire. This mystery. I feel like it in your tongue, too: *ich möchte weinen.* I want this wine[2] that flows in your tongue, I have this strange delight. This desire to take pleasure in my sadness. My thirsty heart wants some of the wine that's asleep on the subterranean tablecloth. I've just wept. It was delicious. I thought I had died and been revived. Before my moistened eyes the world had never been so desirable. I wept very far, all the way to India. The world I do not go to with you is so beautiful. I wept all the way to Tibet where I will go without you, with you in me.

I am a little drunk.

I am a little happy: the breathtaking happiness of having you to lose wells up in my eyes. Go away, Isaac, I'll replace you with tears. You may leave: I'm going to write.

I've already written: "You might go away . . ."

What a day! I can't do anything about it. It must be swallowed. I am haunted by a woman who was abandoned two thousand years ago in another life. I could exorcise her. I bear her. Because she makes me taste the fire that I myself do not light. And I, too, in two thousand years I will haunt a woman with my foreign accents. From where does this woman come to me? From a contralto voice. My incomprehensible secret: I succumb to the song of the contralto: I hear it directly with the marrow in my bones. Even dead I will hear it still.

Isaac, I warn you, before you there was this contralto. Before you I burned, I cursed, and I forgave. Isaac, when you go away, with your hand that removes the earth itself as it withdraws, she curses you, the other one, and it is I who forgive you, I to whom you give this woman to love.

At the end of Saturday I turn on the light; the antique nostalgia abruptly goes out. I just have the time to jot down the last measures of a verse.

At the end of the sentence the tone is going to change.

I forget what I've just said. A little further on the miracle of forgetting awaits me.

Listen: I can go as far as to forget you. Listen to this:

there is not a single umbilical cord that I haven't cut with my teeth. I have delivered asters. And see me now, passed over, effortlessly, onto another moon. Here, all is cold. *I* am acclimatized. What admiration I have for us, who pass from one extremity to the other. We lie down in one book, we get up in another book. As if twenty years had passed. I continue in another key.

In this chapter, the person we love most in the world, whom we think we love and love most in the world when she absents and distances herself, see her exiting our horizon, exiting entirely and so much so that we forget her, we suffer no more from her absence than if we had never loved her, than if we had never made love together. There is no scar. Silence.

Nothing can compare to this absence of suffering, of presence and absence, if not precisely nothing,

she leaves, she takes a plane, the plane takes her, carries her to another continent—the continent of separation?—no, of nonknowledge, no, of indifference, no,

it is we who are carried three thousand kilometers beyond ourselves, in the perfect weightlessness

and we continue to live as if no one had gone, and naturally without noticing it at all,

at such a speed do we turn, at such a distance from yesterday do we not sense it, we lose in weight but we gain in size,

nothing weighs on us, nothing tires us, we write in a lawless improvisation, pages sprout before our eyes, pages that wouldn't sprout on earth sprout like plants, without verticality,

nothing weighs on our thoughts, we jot down, without fear of doing so poorly, the wild vibrations of the world of passions, it must be done in spite of the characters, I read openly, in the joyless drunkenness that the absence of a mirage, that the radioelectric secrets of souls provoke in me, time passes far from us with its billows and its clouds, and sometimes we think of that strange foreigner,

sometimes we think she is in the other world, and, by the way, it is through her that we know another world exists, into which the people we love most in the world pass during our lifetime, in this world.

Like a fish that would like to travel above ground to see how things occur would have to don a diving suit and change its point of view,

I am a fish in a space suit and I observe you astrophysically. With my purity I see your purity. As we will be alive when we are dead, differently alive, I can almost see it from atop this pure absence of suffering. There is no parasite. I have never known such a pure, such a light forgetting. I could almost meet you tomorrow for the first time and by chance.

———————

This is how I got as far as to no longer suffer. I was three thousand kilometers away from all nervous sensation. In a detachment that, to my knowledge, has no name. The thought of returning does not exist. I forgot you, I was three thousand years away from you. I was virgin. I was perfection.

———————

But let her return, this person, this perturbation, and, instantly, no more space suit. Instantly, we tolerate not a minute of distraction, not the least delay. The clock resumes command. What time is it, what time is it, we suffocate. The telephone hasn't rung. I was sure of it, I knew it, I've known it for thirty years, I've been expecting this instant, this flight, I've seen the sails redden at the limit of the visible, for more than thirty years, I predicted it, I wrote it, we've loved each other for thirty years, year after year, leaving each other finding each other, losing each other finding each other and affirming to each other year after year that we will go on seeking and finding each other until the ninetieth year and each year we believe it—

One fine day, suddenly, we don't return. At our return, there is no return. Without warning. It was not the marrow and the bones. And all the books we have written, the poems and essays, suddenly bear diabolical witness against us. I don't even know anymore which of my books this was in.

A telephone that doesn't ring gives rise: I immediately indulge in an orgy of horror, waiting not even a quarter of an hour. If you knew what I do. I open up my demons' cage. In the blink of an eye: havoc. A field burns. I recount the infidelity, the indifference, the inequality of feelings, all this with large brush strokes and without details. (I don't want details, they're insignificant. I want epic songs and smoke.) Quickly cold seizes the earth. The sea has already receded. Last, love dries out and falls to dust. Just barely have I finished my ogress's meal when the telephone rings. On her side, nothing has burned. On mine I quickly note the last incendiary gleams.

How for thirty years I have secretly tasted all the forbidden fruits, how I have recounted to myself betrayals, transgressions, abandonments, later later I shall tell you how. I wouldn't want to live without experiencing malice. I read Dostoyevsky greedily but it wasn't for me. I want my claws, my fangs. I make love with the devil so as to conceive my woman's nightmares. I stuff myself with bitterness, I am of a limitless injustice. This is how I feed my animals: with our venerated flesh, one day I shall tell you how.

The cruelty that licks its chops in my stories, I owe it to us, I hurt myself on you, I snag myself on your sharp edges, I strangle myself with your silences, you are the rope for hanging me (that too, that too, I swing my feet beneath the tree of Yelabouga, all women do), I throw myself from your window, without telling you, behind your back suicide takes me in its delirious arms, I kill myself for you, otherwise, how would I paint my vertigoes? I invent nothing, I copy the horror in truth. One day when I will be too old to be judged and condemned I will reveal to you the worst of my secrets, I will reclaim my rights to my works of brimstone and sign my own roarings myself. But I invent nothing: truly do I bleed.

And while awaiting this day, my love, I go where I cannot go, without telling you, protecting you with my silent body against my own sword blows.

Sleep well, don't wake up, I'm protecting you, but let me pass through you to get to the worst.

In three houses we live, we inhabit three houses, we sleep, we dream, and love pierces through the beds, with its four different petals at whose heart is a sword. Between the three houses, silence is stretched. We never speak of this silence. It is sacred. We don't approach it. We pretend not to hear it. Between the three houses, its nets are stretched. Inside, so many wings, so many cries are caught. We never speak of this. Which doesn't stop silence from playing a sacred music in us. I've been to your house, where I've never been, to all of your houses, in tens of thousands of dreams.

Without modesty without fear without limit in tens of thousands of dreams, I've scoured with curiosity the three foreign houses, I have easily seen a thousand, I met you outside myself in rooms where you glow as no one ever manages to glow in reality, not even *you,*

and I've taken into my parenthesis arms the human being in its entirety, including women, girls, lovers, desires, demons, there is no one I haven't included in my parentheses' arms, and I myself have lived in this marvelous limitless space, but who was I, going farther and wider than me, myself passing among me

I was the other planet, where we all meet each other

I was the time when *I* am not, I am the night that is the place of my greatness

without fear and without modesty, and without ever saying it. In tens of thousands of dreams I have included everything, understood everything, and loved everything, carnally. It was the truth and I wasn't afraid.

Only reality has frightening us as its goal. In truth we are never afraid to love further than in reality, further than love, greater than ourselves.

It is because I have lost you and believed you to be lost and found again so many times, Isaac, that everything is so much given to me.

In the end will I also lose the word *lose*? And then I will find it again, turned to pearls in another tongue.

In one of Clarice's notebooks (in French):

. . . You give me the place, you give me the departure, but then, Isaac, I leave you, I go up to where I no longer know either you or me or anyone.

So if the telephone rings I do not answer, I do not hear it, I'm not expecting you, I do not meet you.

If this is a betrayal, I translate the word *betrayal:* I'm nursing. Luckily, I have more than ten breasts. Because this time I'm feeding a late-born child and the head of a man I did not love twenty years ago but who has preserved a certain beauty, at the same time as I'm carrying a woman in my fluvial arms, a woman so big with song that in feeding her, I am fed.

If this is a betrayal, I ask to be judged in my entirety. I will come with all my lives and all my words. I have found infinite numbers of them. And each word: a body. I ask that I be told how many I am, how much I owe. I will pay in cash, in stars.

When I read your poems, Isaac, I love carnally your bodies far from you . . .

Purified of all hope, they had nothing but flames to expect of themselves. They existed. Here reigns the flamboyant present. All is present. The past? Wasn't erased. Added itself to the present. The past: surrounded them like a magnificent, thirty-year-long train.

They were not born for the strange life—it had befallen them from the sky. Then they discovered its laws. Next they disobeyed its laws, they trembled and regretted for years. They called it prison, they made attempts to escape. But one can't exit one's own soul.

They can no longer lose each other: they live at the heart of loss, which is not what we think. They never lacked desires. Desire is not what we think. Desire is the burning body pregnant with reality. Is the illuminated flesh of reality.

I love your absence. The world is the receding, shining space between my body and your body. Distance yourself, distance yourself, stretch me, stretch my shining body, stretch me as far as the Orient.

Seeing is only one imagination: they see each other every day. Behind the eyelids, where presence and absence dazzle equally. You absent woman, absent man, you long time and far away and equally, the world is in exaltation.

Ah, we have understood down to our entrails that it is the tree of uplifted arms that makes the sky, and that absence is the luminous flesh of presence.

—————

I wonder if we have the right to dream in place of reality, or if that is a crime we commit against our near and dear.

Because without Dreams, Clarice does not exist. Better yet, or worse: without Dreams, she does not love.

It is from Dreams that light, strength, courage, and gaiety come. She lives by dint of Dreams. Dreams are her maternal grandmother. And also her aunt Rachel, the one who laughed while she died.

Her life's need is to find him (Isaac) in her dreams, that's all she thinks about, it is her personal sorcery. That is to say, to have him as Titan of her dreams, as carrier of her earth; to blend him, to mix their flours together to make her dreams; to lose him for five years, to spend five years losing him and in the end to find him again in a dream, a single five-year-long dream, I mean a true dream; and in the same way to lose him for five years and to spend five years in the gloomy gleam of this perdition, and for five years to see the world in saffron colors, to write saffron-colored books, and in the end to find him again in reality as in a dream: with the magic brusqueness of dreams that cuts the cord and unhangs us, whereas we are already dead, and in that very instant five years of terror vanish; I mean a true reality, but in color, the dreamy weight in weightlessness, the dreamy slowness in speed.

In truth could I tell the truth? Theirs? This is a poet's truth: it darts before my eyes, I want to stare it down, it is no longer in my field of vision, it slips beneath my thoughts; I sense it, but I cannot say it: how Clarice's body, if dreamless, would be dead, I don't know how to say this, but I know it.

I also know: when she dies, at the end of her book, it will be from the death of Dreams.

From blessed Great Poverty gush visions, ecstasies, prophecies. Blessed be never, without which she would have never found the path to the faraway, she tells herself. Blessed be never, without which never would the wheat of Dreams have grown so strong.

It is only after many years, among which were years of anger, others of perdition, highs, lows, fires, would-be escapes, ice, metamorphoses, that they saw where they were taking place: in a story. Story for three voices—Clarice's, Isaac's, and the voice of the story that was telling them. Story that they were not writing . . .

Neither one nor the other would have written such a story: it was even the opposite of the ones Clarice wrote. Never would Clarice have invented such a subterranean story, and one that lasted for so many scores of years.

A story whose authors they weren't, they who had written scores of stories, and that would never be either written or published: that is why they feared and loved it. It was for three voices, with contretemps.

"I have the impression," Clarice said cautiously, "that for months now we have been in a new chapter." But Isaac, no, he wasn't. Story with nonsynchronized chapters and several tones. She is in the red tones while he is in the blues.

In *The Train Departure* it is Angela who tells of Angela and Eduardo. In The Train Departure written by Eduardo, the train left a long time ago, Angela didn't take it, she didn't leave, there was no departure.

I forgot to say: never did they say that bread-like sentence to each other: "I love you." In no language? In none. This sentence "I love you" was: the one they didn't say. The unsaid, the inaudible respiration above which their conversations rose. The one that all the other sentences carried on their backs like a golden powder. They don't feel it. Nonetheless, the powder is their mission. Even in the café?

Not even in the café. The other sentences had carried it on their backs. They had begun by not saying it. Not in those words.

―――――――――

At these words (I who have read this far without objecting to adventure), at these words a dark disturbance invades me. Haven't I, following the author, descended below human life? Am I not in that bombed-out field at the earth's northern extremity, where arrive the dead we recall whenever we miss the living?

To live from so little, isn't that a sin? against need and against hunger? Sin against us, beings of the human sort? And against my mother who brings me trays of vegetables arranged like paintings and asks me: what is this book about? Mouth full, I cannot answer. I mumble: about authors.

―――――――――

Isaac: I don't love you, this creation only concerns the two of us. Let them give me some other word than the word *love.* Let them give me the key to my foreign country.

No, I do not love you. It is a question of inner habitation. Of a house with inhabitants. You (are) me.

I don't love you. I have the world inhabited by you *(translated from the German).*

―――――――――

On the balcony trumpet my hibiscus, which were given to me. My traveling companions in those very desert places. A story without hibiscus? I think of the goodness in being loved on this earth with flowers. And of champion fasters, who exert their enchantment over the author. I crunch on a crust of fresh bread. And let no one tell me that Clarice, who loves fresh bread, doesn't regret never hearing the word that gives and saves, because I won't believe it. Today I cannot swallow this story without anguish.

I miss the author: I'd like to know how this is going to end before reading on.

I know, I know, I said I didn't want to get mixed up with her anymore. Not for years to come.

But sometimes we say farewell to each other forever and then we telephone each other four days after the farewell. We're no longer in the secret.

Anyway, I'm merely expressing a desire and my uneasiness, since I don't know where the author is.

I'll continue reading, then, in the most troubled tumult of uncertainty:

Clarice: Another word from the word *love,* my love: what's involved is this labor at the extreme, ultimate limit of thought. Old opacified thought must be pierced. And to that end, ridding oneself of words that clutch with their thousands of tiny frightened fingers at our feet, our knees, our eyelids, begging us to not go forward. No farther. And that hold us back and tell us the worst, the wan, dull, chilly, earthly version of the human condition. Ridding ourselves of the words that separate us from the world, and utter their cries of dread, and are made for dissuading us from attaining and leaving, and touching and surpassing and tasting all that is promised us in this world, and for making us believe that all isn't good, that isn't good, this is good, for mystifying and petrifying us, and separating us from the wholly good world. We must become splendid again. Once upon a time we suckled at the tangled roots of Nature.

Sucked the sweetness of bitterness. We knew how to seize within suffering the extreme taste of life. We were once free and powerful, we don't even know anymore where or when. All that happened to us: thanks. When were we generous? When were we not dupes of fear? When did we make of a minute an occasion for the greatest, the finest, the epoch for a journey with wedding, feast, construction of a palace and big orange lights? We used to know how. When did we play all the instruments? Between language and us there was neither obedience nor disobedience, only exact conjugation of feeling and music. Saying didn't crush. When did we still extract from the dough of words hoped-for, unique, necessary accents?

When did we naturally live very high up, and very deeply, and now we look at the above from below and call it impossible and superhuman so as to protect our acquired lowness, our laziness, our meagerness of imagination?

We haven't always been so subhumanly human, so established, so greedy, so reduced in soul and so fat in stomach, and mistaken the soul for the stomach, and feared hunger every day.

In some other time we were, evidently, happy and effortless, we have forgotten but the nights remember, we didn't compare "a lot" with "a little," "how much" didn't exist, we went along without counting, we knew how to take pleasure from heaviness and lightness, losing was a find, each sensation a benediction, each instant a master, each hunger celebration of bread, when we lived naturally, supernaturally. And no complaint, only a marvelous curiosity.

I had the power. Women who saw me pass admired the promise of my back. I, too, felt my wideness glitter. I know how to carry the world. On the ocean's shores, worries sprout. I face my country, my unknown, my future, my book. How to enter, coming from this shore and without passport, and without papers? And without swimsuit for entering the sea. I am before words. I possess the unknown power of myself, which is nakedness. I plunge. The dive is so forceful it carries me a long way without weakening above the waters' surface, without ever breaking it, for a long time I skim the waters like a giant swallow. In truth I fly. Unwearied, wingless. My back, my body are my very wings, and in my body: endless desire and destiny. I'll get there, I'll get there. I don't let anything stop me, neither illusion of ocean nor illusion of words. Let's go to the world's shore, and let's know how to.

When did we fall into the old net of poisonous words, and, at a single stroke, farewell to our gaiety, our genius, our powers!

And as far back as the memory of our fall. And we think we were fetuses in the net, born for armor and hindrance. We get up without eternity, and one hour later we have retired from great adventures. We exist with our eyes on the eyes of clocks. We won't follow passing Beauty, we won't jump into the stream, we'll flee the abyss, we'll be blind, deaf, and tired, our dreamless back docile. The book of the world? a dictionary, everything is in the dictionary, loving is in the dictionary, everything is put away, described, dictionaried, known, my body is in the dictionary,

oh my love, we are in the monster's maw, and it has thirty-five thousand teeth

I've just looked up the verb *love* in the dictionary, and I can confirm for you that it is not with *love* that I love you, with love also, but not only with known *love* and its known synonyms,

no, my loving is not that loving. That lot is not a lot. I look up *ladder* and I don't find my ladder, the one that sprouts according to my élan, with each élan a new branch.

If we no longer have the grace of our native height, let's plant the vegetable ladder and climb back up. I stand up, I lift my foot—and already I'm in the other world. We are always much stronger than we think.

I hear my own cry of joy rise up in the space sprouting anew around my heart. I don't know what I'm writing to you. I am: following the movement. I am: following the ladder. I am sure. I have defected: gone over to life. I go forth: into happiness. I don't look all around me or into the eyes of the clock: happiness. I do not think, I respond. I am called to life and I respond.

Who says this happiness isn't happiness? Who counts my eternity in hours? Who judges my written work, who grades my infinite, who pretends to take my measurements? I am not answerable to your University. At school, I'm a zero.

Who's frowning? Who summons me to the butcher's and, head down, I show up, my book bag under my arm, without knowing the subject?

It is: "Death" with all her synonyms, derived and sent, her paper soldiers, and her allies, our unimaginable lack of imagination and the tyranny of our lack of imagination. It is Death and her fakers.

"Death," what a story! And to think we invented her, invented her so well we don't even know anymore that we are ourselves the authors of her stories. We who extracted her from our weakness, painted and crowned her so as to assure weak days for our weakness. Next we arm her with all the words that diminish us. The miracle is that we invented "God" and that we feel so glad to have done so. The antimiracle is that we invented "Death."

And the mystery is that we mix up inventing and believing. We invent this word *Death* and the word becomes our master, yet we do not disinvent? One word, and see how crippled, stiff, and crooked we are, and for years. Its strength is in its weakness. The enemy is almost invisible: do we distrust a word? And behold how it stings, in one thousandth of a second, our myriad neurons; one second later, poisoned messages travel our nerve endings, and one minute later we are dyed and mortalized down to our smallest state of mind.

And besides, what an ugly word: *Death*. To die for a word? At least let it be magical, and let it ring at God's door, like the word *Absinthe* or the word *Mystical*. At least a bright silver horse, or a star with singing hair. This life in exchange for the white pebble that carries our new names engraved on it, but nothing less. Or else the word *missed* in the feminine front and back: I missed you, I didn't miss you, a word that is missing no éclat: this tear, suspended from my eyelashes and ripening, your name murmured by my eyes.

Today I'm taking on words that bite, our ancient, enemy inventions. It is Friday, day for major cleaning, I'm going to pass my tongue through a fine-toothed comb. And purify and scratch the floor and walls and ceiling of my brain, this is an exhausting labor, one must turn against oneself, one must lie in wait for, surprise, trick oneself. And watch out, because the words return at the least distraction. I'm going to make a mistake. But I know it. I'm going to suspect myself of cheating. For as long as is necessary. I will never disarm. To start with I don't make a mistake: I've decided to break with *Death*. It is a very simple war. There's a battlefield.

What an enormous cosmic show! we are there by the hundred millions, ready for the exams. By waves of generations. And we are given ration tickets for life. But *I* was not born on this scrap of paper. In 1789, it is already said in the streets, we were born free to be millennial. Against us the fatigue that wants "a cessation of life" (I found that in the dictionary). But already no longer against. For we leave the battlefield immediately. Behold our way of waging war: leaving. My river has changed beds. Death? We no longer believe in her: we cut off her supplies, her life source. It's enough to think about doing it. Everything is the work of beliefs. With one belief we fashion death. With one belief we open the portals of time: behold, each minute is accorded us according to our desire.

You, poor Death that I attack, I don't resent you, creature of our anxieties, enormous fantasy that we've carved on the wall of nightmares, so as to venerate you afterward with hate, monster child of our entrails, in whom we swear we'll see our assassin, strengthless thing, carried on a fiery throne, fruit of our palenesses, poor divinity that we fashion in the image of our fears and our illnesses, tortured bit of lace, innocent character that we pierce with blows, you whom we beg to help us live softly, live somberly, live slowly, squeezed into tiny shoes, and to whom we dedicate stacks of smoking lies, how will I forget you, obedient ferociousness whom we pretend to obey.

No, Death, you are not this—this set of dragon's dentures. You may go in peace, you may melt away. Go, I don't need to bump up against you in order to live and revive.

————————

I've gone out. Before me the field of time: everything is to be cultivated. I must announce this. It is, all the same, a change in kind. The universe must be rewritten. I don't yet know how: freely, vertically, descending. Trumpets!

————————

Voice of Clarice to voice of Isaac: —I've just effectuated a break with *Death*. This is not a game. We must purify the word. Are you listening to me?

Voice of Isaac: —I listen to you, I obey you.

Voice of Clarice: —These shivers—these nights inside the day, these falling stars and organs we call "death": they are only seeking flesh. Life itself crying out for help. So if we call this hunger, this moment of hollow belly "you," we will suffer from joy. I feel a great joy blowing, coming to me from the world: it is the absence of fear that inspires the inner landscape. The world and I, we laugh.

Should I be afraid of losing you? I am sole author of the threat: I have my own betrayals to fear, my absences of mind, my decenterings. Yesterday when you phoned me, I wasn't on your level. I was beneath the ground, halfway buried in my own silence, far from our territory, in slowness, seeking the root of a sensation, when you called me. And, lack of strength and speed, I didn't succeed in rising to your level. I saw you clearly, me up to my neck in darkness. I spoke to you with my mouth and throat, the rest of my body in silence. Such is a mute animal's pain: you hold out your hand to me. And my hand does not obey me. It is a beast. It takes me five minutes to rouse it. When it finally returns and I hold it out, your hand is gone. Living us demands of me the strongest of my strengths. I am in the challenge. I am the challenge. I fear not succeeding at our minutes. Living is my concern. But dying? It will happen to us, I'll tell you about it. I already know I'll have to fight as never before in order to rise to the level of this very high moment. I want to get there. I will.

Thirty years ago, I would have never thought that we would have this millennial work to do. I was without fatality. Would I have been afraid?

———————

Voice of Isaac: —The fatality came later. It is what happened to us. Living, what suffering! What suffering! (he says, with, in his voice, a burst of gaiety). Pleasure is so exacting. Over there, what will we become?

Voice of Clarice: —For future I want the tree of life. I

175

don't know what it is, or if it is a tree that resembles a tree, or perhaps the planet's heartwood.

Voice of Isaac: —For future I want—a future.

Voice of Clarice: —In the future's future we will invent a still more ideal story. With another word from the word *we*. With other "words" than our words, unknown words, in music colors.

———————

They had been living in this story for thirty years now, as they wrote: by keeping silences kept by silences. From which escaped flames.

And then one day . . . one day, one year, after thirty years, comes the unexpected.

And so one summer Clarice's silence quavered: all of a sudden, like a gaze opening in a dark wood, the desire to say the never-before-said words trembled inside her. Trembled and then rippled, rippled and then flowered. But why so suddenly, after so many years, and why had it never been awakened before?

For this. She wanted to say what had never been said, because the sentence was so simple, so ordinary. Because after thirty years there is no more error, or calculation, all is of a great purity, she tells herself. Who knows, perhaps it is the desire to say something that has become extraordinary. The sentence would loom up from the shadows like a wink from God. A nothing, but solemn and brilliant. A crystal triumph.

And after so many many years she has the vague desire to lose something, that which she had kept, in order to surrender it, to render it up, to God, to nature, to noise. And she wanted something she didn't really want: to sacrifice the sacrifice, because it was behind this long silence. She wanted the other side of this silence. Its extremity. What created the sentence was this silence. She wanted to hear the sentence's long silence ("I love you," the name of God). For a whole week inside her, the taut string of a mute violin. A sob wept in secret. And desire for a singular orange. And to drink the sun. And then to blaspheme: because it is blasphemy that consecrates the sacred. Will I live my whole life without ever having said this sentence? —Wait another thirty years.

A whole life with this sentence silenced, like the children one has promised oneself not to have, and instead of children one has the children one doesn't have. Tomorrow, tomorrow,

each day the desire grows. It was no more than a question of hours. And suddenly, it was now. It was night, there was no more wall, or edge, or dam, or past, or consideration, only the breath of the sentence in her lungs, and as one opens a window to free a butterfly, she said:

"You know I love you," like a piece of eternal, gentle news, with the very low voice of someone who chants the first notes of a long, complex revelation.

"You know I love you," and the butterfly casts itself into the night, I throw "you know I love you" at you, as one casts oneself toward a star, by falling with all one's might.

Because what she wanted was to hear the music. The sentence expects no response

It was to herself she addressed herself: you know yes I know, surprising herself, at the edge of time, and she watched it roll along its starry stream.

But behold: the listening voice has let itself slip into the speaking voice, and "me, too" she murmured, but so low that no one heard her, if not the starry stream of time.

It was midnight. Thirty years had passed. Clarice wept. She had spent in one fell swoop thirty years of pearls and prophecies. Wept, but so delicately that no one heard her except me. She could never say it again. All of a sudden there was a past to what had never been but present. The sentence shattered their eternity. A slight blow of the ax to the middle, and now through the fissure filtered time. I didn't want to say it. There was a ripening of silence. "I love you," I said, because I couldn't help myself. Behind me, an enormous night came to a close.

"I'll never tell you again," she promised. Who knows if in thirty years the sentence won't have regained its magic silence? And if the dawns and nights will breathe it anew among the trees?

At the end of summer, Isaac wrote the poem:

Um zerstört zu sein.

With his voice of sad young silk he recited the lines to her, on the phone.

With his crumpled voice, foreboding and regret intermingled, that she secretly loved more than himself: voice of the poet who is the beggar, the vanquished, in which she recognized her own hoped-for defeats, voice of divine impotence. In truth this God can do nothing for Creation, except extend an ear. The syllables fell upon her from a high, veiled silence, coming from the troubled blue of poetry, coming from the German tongue, for which she felt an intimate nostalgia, for a long time coming from this German star, from which, for her, revelations escaped. Spoken words of before and after us. (But it was in hard Brazilian, in the rocky resistant dough, that she carved the musicless paths of her own tales. She: writing with flint, he: with violin and piano.)

Came the poem:

Um zerstört zu sein	So as to be destroyed
um wieder aufgebaut zu sein	so as to be rebuilt
ist der Tempel gebaut	is the Temple built

Beneath the voice the two of them, Clarice and Isaac, bend their heads so as to better hear its accents vibrating in the invisible branches, in the darkness.

She felt herself plunged, fully dressed, into the oldest of rivers.

—You are in me like the world's forgiveness, she said with inexactitude, but the agitated intensity of her voice said the rest: she thought she had lost the world, all the golden threads broken, it was falling, it was rolling, she could already see the empty cavity—she had just been pardoned. With the world's hollow still in her eyes, but in her throat the sob of the revived. We weep for ourselves with joy, not knowing how to celebrate—by laughing more humbly—"the rebuilding."

All is so as to, *alles ist um*. She lived. The first breath after a month of constricted throat. Blood returns to the stone. I'm hungry. I know how to swim between the clouds.

She hung up. The doors to the world turned on their hinges, behind the mountains' shoulder. The poem was taking effect. At the first words she saw, from the sky broken open like an egg, flow an unending hemorrhage of stars—

by the next line the world's vein no longer bleeds, the wound closes up, forests rise on the earth like women, innocent, after a bad dream. Books open, the dead dress in haste and without ulterior motive. It's going to be time for breakfast. A festive spirit blows. Those who have suffered dry their eyes. Forgetting is forgotten.

Nothing bad can happen, she thought, that time will not transform into seeds of another wheat.

Today begins again. Day of first stone and first meal after the destruction. A golden joy dilates the celestial breast: it is the sun rising in my breast. This small woman who reascends the century with a lively step despite her age, and despite the slowness of the snow, is Clarice, the great-grandmother I never knew: I recognize her by my eyes, which are hers. Farthest from my right shoulder, three generations away, I see the silver-sandaled shadow slip away, who in three generations will carry my name.

All is so as to, and all is for.

Oh if we could die more than once. She would have easily made a round-trip.

Something had happened to her this summer: she had never been so happy. There was no reason. It was the summer of 1977, and she was happy. Amid the familiar fear and the familiar separation, and despite the regret and impatience that never go out, light passed.

As if she had arrived. In her country. Yet there was no country? But no lack of country either. Unexpected happiness, almost out of place. Hers, passing through him, but unshared. As if there were suddenly a roof, a bed, a terrace on the sea, a table, shared—everything there wasn't. This summer, everything is enough for her and satisfying to her. A country is being created inside her

She had unknown appetites: the sudden desire to write ten books "at the same time," ten different books, but fruits of the same summer, to have ten hands, or perhaps ten voices, because, there before her, the world was superabundant, never had there been so many bursts to pluck, and without explanation. And the desire to never again stop writing, one book driving up to the next book's door, she no longer saw any reason at all to stop, since the path went on. Which had never happened to her before: because up until now, long absences of body would stretch between her books. She would hibernate. Until a dream came along to tear her open.

But this summer the unexpected happens to her: she no longer senses an end approaching. The back door is open. From inside her book she already sees the first meters of the next. Its ground very different. She desires it in advance, she has a premonition of the first outstretched hand, the wordless emotion of the first contact, so slight, so cautious, the first heart pang, and immediately afterward the first lines, this indissoluble union between the finite and the infinite, between the existing and the nonexisting, this hand-to-hand battle happening in a single body, this exhausting invention of each fistful of earth, each mouthful of air. It didn't exist at all, she hadn't even thought about it, and yet she heard it breathing just "after." What impatience drives her this summer!

She was pregnant at the age of fifty-eight, and, naturally, like all women in this state, she was laughing, laughing. Pregnant? With mystery. Without knowing what would be born, she was already in transformation: she had grown. Her shoulders widened: perhaps I'll have to carry an earth? Her body slightly colossal. According to her body: what was brewing would demand of her her greatest strength. She let it come.

Strength that gave her a taste for devouring. Or perhaps: for being devoured. A voracity takes her as its object. And hunger of the ear also. Summer when, if she had been God, she would have lit musics all over the world. No gestation, genesis, she feels it down to her entrails, in the silence. God was the first to yell loudly in his language while he worked.

One day I'm going to wake up speaking a completely foreign language. She was laughing, laughing. And her shoulders were wider, and she was copper colored, and sparkling. I'm expecting an event that wants me athletic.

Next, she thought a lot about the end of their story. Since no one will ever tell it. As an author who is passionate about her art, she thinks about the "last chapter": the most unimaginable of all the chapters in the world. She couldn't even begin to approach it. This is why she was attracted: she is a great, night peacock circling around a light, and going mad in a forest of reflections. She thinks a lot about the book of their fatality, which, together and apart, they do not write. We are truly characters in a book: blind people reunited by a Desire that surpasses them. I would have liked—to read it. It is this one, of course, swinging like a dazzling apple in the middle of a distant garden. Ah, if I could see it. She guesses, she leans, she still sees—a few chapters, then nothing more. A fog, an effacement of space. It's too early, she thinks. Perhaps in thirty years.

She dreams often of "blank pages." All is annulled. She doesn't have the law degree she has. She begins again. She shows up in a state of absence. What has never happened to her in life is going to happen to her. Happened to her. Time passes before her, she doesn't write a thing. There is no door. She doesn't enter. Before her: long, white, expectant leaves of paper. Not a sound. Not a line. An itch, a roar, a cry, a snore, oh no, neither a horse, nor a pig, nor a mouse, there is no one. The boat is expecting. She is expecting. Two silences, oh no, a single silence. The leaf of paper expects an answer, Clarice doesn't have it. She cannot beg. She knows not where she is. She could flee. She cannot. The page is her page. The whiteness is her whiteness. Flee, who will know? At the bottom of the long gaping leaf, she could read her pale name written in pencil: Clarice Lispector, it's her all right. She is, letter by letter. White letter addressed to her? She didn't understand. Her fortune-teller says to her: "What has never happened before? And could never happen to you? And is happening to you?" This was the enigma. No explanation.

She loved this summer of incomprehension: only came to her things that couldn't happen. So what's going to happen to me? This summer, from where would the mystery come? Its blow? Because it's coming. To me, addressed in pencil, almost unreadable. (She is on the lookout.) Or else the woman who sent me this double leaf of paper, impossible to fill, with all this empty space, is, already,

(She put her glasses on)
She sees:
(*I* don't see a thing)
She writes. What does she write? She writes: Ah!

—Where is the author?! I shouted.

All of a sudden I have a tremendous feeling of nostalgia for the author. I can no longer do without her. I'm cold. I'm worn out. I've lost density by reading. We're approaching a too-rare zone. I need the author in order to get to the end. I run to fetch her.

I found her. It wasn't easy, in the surface state I was in. I had to crawl for a long time in order to forge a path to the interior; it is the body itself that is the path.

The author is on the mountain. She's returned. She got there before me. Forewarned? It's her book.

—What's going on? I say.

—I don't know a thing. It happens above me. I'm anxious.

She follows the story taking place now up on the mountain. It is the mount of metamorphoses, where Clarice has caracoled. I recognize it. All is imaginary. A bit immaterial. The author, nervous, standing, notes in the dark. (It is night.) Words come to her. I want to see. I crawl up the cliff, like a cat wedding the arid rock. Once up there I can't see a thing. It's farther up. Does the end happen up there?

In the effort to seize the dark revelation, the author burns up all her inner forces. A dust of fire notes.

And all of a sudden, the author draws herself up violently, as if she has seen the angel of the forbidden.

"What am I doing—here?" She gets scared and takes off running. "I must stop," she decides, "if it's time to," running and wondering how this would end, she had no idea, but feared

the mountain is dark as night, the ground rolls beneath my feet, the mountain descends along with me,

—I was wrong, I shouldn't have returned, because at the end of everything is death, what day is it? she shouts,

—August 30th—

—"Ah!" As if I had struck her.

And all along the way, the ground uncertain, the landscape hazy, darkness grows, I see less and less, of the world, only direction remains, up down, the door, the door

I cross the earth running

she, the author, with a lightness of thought, descends faster and faster, wondering if one could not imagine a book that would have no end,

running down very steep stairways as if she didn't feel the steps, and far ahead of me, a hundred steps ahead, I hear her voice

—I mean to say that would only stop because at page 250 we *must* stop, this is where the reader's getting off, day breaks, night takes off with our dreams, and—

—wait for me! I cried. I couldn't go any faster. I shouldn't follow this foolish madwoman, who once again distances me from myself, but I do it, rising to the challenge, she is farther and farther away,

—and thus, she pursues, with all due speed, as if she wanted to get to the world's exit before the cock's crow,

and me, in the panic I've just lost my right shoe

—because if I manage to exit this book before the end of the summer of 1977, perhaps there will be no last chapter,

—see, this is what she has been looking for all her life, a book with, at the end, something else, flowers perhaps

—red, she says, or a dream, yes, a dream, since we never know if a dream is not perhaps a door leading to reality, always running, hundreds of steps ahead of me,

—and there is never any end within a dream

And isn't this what Clarice and Isaac requested—that they never be awakened—

And at the same time congratulating herself: I found, I see the end of the book without end, it is the magic end, I'm going to note it, I'm going to exit, wake myself up (but always running, she didn't make it to the awakening, the dream protects her and her characters, in fact, the dream intended to set her down on the other shore only at the book's end—because after the last page—)

I can see the ends of the earth, I descend quickly to the foot of the wall, where is she, before me I see two closed doors, two eyelids in the limitless wall, I open the one on the right, she isn't there, I open the other, she's not there anymore

—in that moment the cock crows, in reality it is a squirrel singing in my tree, and I never see her again, I only hear echoes of her voice, she becomes confused with the distance, and with those thousands of narrow, empty steps that descend alone and are extinguished beyond the book.

I am alone.

There is no one to finish telling this ideal story. That's fine. I'm going to place some roses and hibiscus—where?

I'm going to make you an avowal: for ten days I've been trying to write a last page for this book. I've written scores. All rejected. The book doesn't want them. One cannot force a book. The door is closed to me. There are books that want our death. Others want our metamorphosis. This one wants my bewilderment, and to never show me the end.

I have nothing more to do with the author. She has truly dropped me. And to think I believed in the beginning that I was, myself, the author's author! In the end was I her character? No, this book has nothing to do with my life—I have let myself be led, contradicted. That is a mistake. But mistakes are a part of truth. Truth contains mistakes, life contains the world, and for a long time I contained the author. And I went all the way to the end.

Last night I saw the end of the author.

Is it your end, world, the end of our beautiful kingdom, that we allow to be fashioned before our eyes? All of us, humanity, watching the earth be prey to malevolent phenomena. Fire gnawed at the victim like a beast, soon it will have eaten the planet. See, it's halfway there. We, humanity, hugging ourselves to the edge of the amputated pancake. The author says: "That's it! It has bitten also at the trees of morning." So I exited absence. "Water!" I shouted. One country after the other dies, uttering cries of flame. And we forget the Water! I start to run. I seize the long red stream lying helplessly on the ground, the one no one among us dreams of waking. And running, shooting, unfurling, I approach the foyer, and I shoot I shoot, at the larvae of fire, I will kill you in the egg, I will nip you in the bud, ah, the water wants to be persuaded, but with all the speed and energy in the world, I manage just the same, I go all through the woods, which burst into sobs: will the world be no more? I water the mountain with its threatened furnaces, no, Fire, I have to kill you, I have to rip my country from your smoking chops. Besides, beyond the inferno, behind your back, idiot, a huge foreign body of water begins to recover the earth. From now on, it will be impossible for the fire to swallow the mountain. Now it is the water that is devouring the scene, coming from where? I lift my head, and I see: the walls bordering the dream's horizon are inundated, it's coming from over there! Countries, flee; if you can leave the earth, fly away, for the globe that was our ground is now nothing but a gigantic mudhole, nauseating and swallowing itself. I see a body of water advancing like an inextinguishable fire; countries, if you can tear yourselves away from this scene, beat your wings, take to the sky, I cried, me, alone, witness, but in vain, to this apocalypse.

Alone. The author—immobile before the earth in dread—didn't she, right this instant, disappear, very clearly, in a sigh behind my ear: "It is too bright, too clear here . . . farewell"

A journey is threatening our existence. We don't get up every day in the same book. In the full of life we are transported to another life. In order to return to ourselves in a month, a year, a country later.

I've just been traveling. I'm at the end.

In the end one always ends up beginning, but in order to end, no (and so many lives take place above us), ending doesn't end a thing . . . . We do not end . . .

I stop the book. I get off. Now I'm going home. Behind me, the loud sound of wings, it has gone . . .

If I were to write a book, I would begin with a garden at dawn, rosy, at the foot of a mountain. I would do absolutely everything to keep the book from turning against me,

to make it go toward the south, toward the rosiness, toward the sea, which are my true directions, if ever it were I who wrote.

Translator's Notes

Translator's Preface

1. "Lutte sourde, plus ou moins sensible, plus ou moins valorisée, par littérature interposée surtout, entre le sujet *donné* et le sujet *surgi.*" Charles Grivel, "Envers de deux. Enfer de deux," in *Du Féminin,* ed. Mireille Calle (Sainte-Foy, Quebec: Les Editions le Griffon d'argile, 1992), 187.

2. Quoted in Lynn Kettler Penrod, "Hélène Cixous: Lectures Initiatiques, Lectures Centrifuges," in *Du Féminin,* 95. Witness, for example, the reading practice of Penrod, who explains that each time she takes up a new text by Cixous, she opens it first to page 25, for she was born on a 25th day. There, she searches for a phrase that will speak especially, secretly to her, and finds she's never disappointed (84).

3. "Force faible" is a phrase from Mireille Calle, "L'Ecrire-penser d'Hélène Cixous," in *Du Féminin,* 102.

4. "Pour nous qui écrivons, ce qui importe c'est le processus. C'est la tempête, c'est le brouillon" (129). (For those of us who write, what's important is the process. It's the tempest, it's the rough draft.) Cixous, "En Octobre 1991 . . . ," in *Du Féminin,* 115–37.

5. Ibid. "Un feu nous prend, nous surprend. L'écriture est loin derrière. Les moments brûlants, comment les saisir? Comment prendre le feu avec les mains?" (122). (A fire seizes us, surprises us. Writing is far behind. How to grab hold of burning moments? How to hold fire with our hands?)

6. Ibid. "C'est vrai, j'ai des problèmes de pronoms toujours" (116). (It's true, I've always had problems with pronouns.)

7. Marta Peixoto, *Passionate Fictions* (Minneapolis: University of Minnesota Press, 1994).

8. Diana Fuss, *Essentially Speaking: Feminism, Nature and Difference* (New York: Routledge, 1989), 52.

9. I think it worth recalling, nearly twenty-five years after the publication of Cixous's invocation, in her essay "The Laugh of the Medusa," that women "write the body," and some fifteen years after the initial Anglo-American discovery and critique of what we on this continent have called "French feminisms," that Cixous, once again in keeping with her ultimate kinship with a long line of poets, is not by any means the first or the only writer to speak of the body as vital source. As Edmond Jabès has said, in an interview with the American novelist Paul Auster, "I do believe that a writer works with his body. You live with your body, and the book is above all the book of your body. . . . A full phrase, a lyrical phrase, is something that has great breath, that allows you to breathe very deeply . . . we work with our bodies, our breathing, our rhythm, and . . . writing in some sense mimes all this." Auster, *The Art of Hunger* (New York: Penguin, 1992), 154–55.

10. Indeed, those who dare to live within this realm of unknowability in reality (as opposed to poetry) often pay with their health, their sanity, or their very lives. Remember, for example, the rape and murder of the transgendered

Nebraskan youth Brandon Teena, killed for her transgressions of gender laws.

11. Cixous, "En Octobre": "Je me dis: heureusement qu'il y a cette voix, cette poésie-philosophie, pour . . . faire vibrer les contradictions" (117). (I tell myself: fortunately there is this voice, this poetry-philosophy, for causing contradictions to vibrate.)

12. Calvin Thomas, *Male Matters: Masculinity, Anxiety, and the Male Body on the Line* (Urbana: University of Illinois Press, 1996).

13. Lispector, *The Stream of Life,* trans. Elizabeth Lowe and Earl Fitz (Minneapolis: University of Minnesota Press, 1989).

14. February 12 is a date that appears numerous times over the years in the Cixousian oeuvre; only here, in her "book of days," does she finally reveal its meaning: it was the date of her father's death.

15. Quoted in Peixoto, *Passionate Fictions,* 59.

16. Willis Barnstone, *The Poetics of Translation: History, Theory, Practice* (New Haven, Conn.: Yale University Press, 1993), 5.

17. Jacques Derrida, *The Post Card: From Socrates to Freud and Beyond,* trans. Alan Bass (Chicago: University of Chicago Press, 1987).

18. See Catherine A. F. MacGillivray, "Translator's Preface," to Cixous's *Manna for the Mandelstams for the Mandelas* (Minneapolis: University of Minnesota Press, 1992).

Introduction

1. The word for "foreignness" in French—*l'étrangeté*—is feminine, hence my use of feminine pronouns "she" and "her" in this sentence. See my preface.

2. The word for "question" in French—*la question*—is feminine, hence the use in English of the feminine pronouns.

3. The word for "suffering" in French—*la souffrance*—is feminine, hence the use in English of the feminine pronouns.

The Main Character of This Book Is . . .

1. In French, "liberty" is feminine, *la liberté,* thus the pronoun "her."

2. In French, "time" is masculine, *le temps,* thus the pronouns "him" and "his."

My Wombs Tombs

1. This is the name of a major avenue in Oran, Algeria.

2. The italicized phrase *"the first unmeeting"* is in English in the French original.

3. In French, "my knowingness" is feminine, *ma science,* thus the second instance of "herself."

Tearing Down the Wall, a Work of Angels

1. See Cixous's *Three Steps on the Ladder of Writing,* trans. Sarah Cornell and Susan Sellers (New York: Columbia University Press, 1993), 3–4, for a discussion of the first letter of Cixous's first name, *H,* pronounced *hache* in French, which means "ax."

2. *The Slaughtered Ox* is a painting by Rembrandt.

3. "Gumzoule Taube" is the phonetic spelling of a Yiddish phrase.

4. In French, the word for "deaths," *les morts,* may also mean "the (masculine) dead."

5. *Les morts,* "the dead," is masculine in French. See note 4.

6. *Mes vies,* "my lives," is feminine in French.

Night My Foreign Life

1. Cixous's references to Penthesilea and Achilles are always references to the characters in the eighteenth-century Prussian writer Heinrich von Kleists's play *Penthesilea.*

2. This is a reference to Kafka.

3. In French, *la phrase* is feminine, hence the use in English of feminine pronouns (see my preface).

4. "She" here refers to "a freedom," which is feminine (*une liberté*) in French.

5. See note 1 to "Tearing Down the Wall, a Work of Angels."

Self-Portraits of a Blind Woman

1. Cixous is referring to the main character in Lispector's novel *The Hour of the Star,* trans. Giovanni Pontiero (New York: New Directions, 1992).

2. Rodrigo is the first-person narrator of Lispector's novel *The Hour of the Star.*

3. This was the day before Lispector's death.

4. Lispector's last novel *The Hour of the Star* ends with Macabea's death beneath the wheels of a car.

5. Cixous is referring to the Rembrandt painting of the same name. She writes of this painting and others by Rembrandt in her essay "Bathsheba or the Interior Bible," trans. Catherine A. F. MacGillivray, *New Literary History* 24, no. 4 (Autumn 1993): 817–36.

6. See ibid.

7. Angela and Eduardo are the two main characters in Lispector's novel *A Lição* (The Lesson).

8. In German, *ander* means "other."

9. Cixous is referring to the way that Pushkin died, from a bullet wound suffered in a duel with a man who was overly attentive to Pushkin's young wife.

10. In French, the last two syllables of the name Alexander, *Alexandre,* sound like *cendre,* the French word for "ash."

11. *Lonza* is Italian for wolf; Cixous is alluding to the allegorical animal that appears in the beginning of Dante's *Inferno.*

12. *The Broken Jug* is a play by the eighteenth-century Prussian writer Heinrich von Kleist.

An Ideal Story

1. *Nie* is "never" in German; *nid* is "nest" in French; they are crosslinguistic homophones.

2. The German verb *weinen,* "to weep," recalls the German noun *wein,* "wine."

Hélène Cixous was born and raised in Oran, Algeria, and later attended university in Paris. She is currently head of the Centre d'Etudes Féminines and professor of English literature at the experimental University of Paris VIII-Vincennes, which she helped to found. Her celebrated seminars attract students of literature and women's studies from the world over and are held at the Collège de Philosophie in Paris. She has also lectured widely in the United States, at the University of California at Berkeley and Irvine, Harvard, and, most recently, at Northwestern University, where she is currently Distinguished Visiting Professor of French. Although best known in North America as a writer of "French feminisms," Cixous is primarily a poet who has published more than thirty-five works in forms as varied as avant-garde fiction, plays (a number of which were especially commissioned by the renowned Théâtre du Soleil), prose poetry, essays, and a hybrid genre that might be called poetic theory. Her most recent publications in France include the fictions *OR, les lettres de mon père* and *Messie,* and the plays *La Ville parjure ou le Réveil des Erinyes* and *L'Histoire (qu'on ne connaîtra jamais).* In 1994, Cixous received France's *Prix de la Critique dramatique* for the best play of the year for *La Ville parjure.*

Catherine A. F. MacGillivray studied with Hélène Cixous at the University of Paris VIII from 1980 to 1984, where she completed a *Licence* and a *Maîtrise* in *Lettres Modernes* and *Etudes Féminines.* She received her doctorate in French literature from the University of California at Berkeley and has taught French, English, and women's studies at Berkeley and Barnard College. Currently, she is an assistant professor of English and women's studies at the University of Northern Iowa. MacGillivray has published translations of a number of Cixous's essays, as well as another of her book-length fictions, *Manna for the Mandelstams for the Mandelas,* published by the University of Minnesota Press in 1992.